OUTLAW TALES

of Washington

True Stories of the Evergreen State's
Most Infamous Crooks, Culprits, and Cutthroats

Second Edition

Elizabeth Gibson

TWODOT®

GUILFORD, CONNECTICUT
HELENA, MONTANA
AN IMPRINT OF GLOBE PEQUOT PRESS

A · TWODOT® · BOOK

Map by Daniel Lloyd © Morris Book Publishing, LLC

Library of Congress Cataloging-in-Publication Data is available on file.

ISBN 978-0-7627-6030-5

Printed in the United States of America

10 9 8 7 6 5 4 3 2 1

Contents

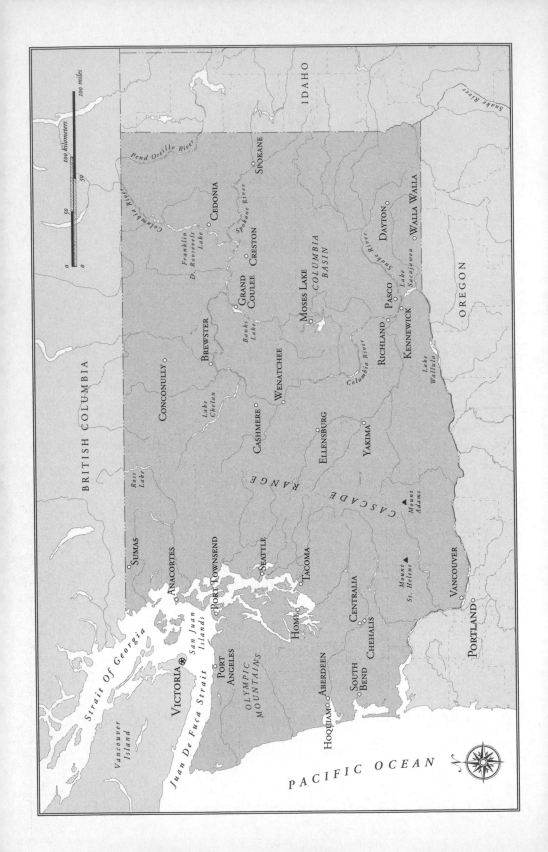

Contents

Introduction

Although explorers landed on the coast of what would become Washington state hundreds of years ago, Washington was one of the last states to have enough population to officially join the United States of America. By the time Washington entered the union in 1889, the Wild West days were coming to a close. Yet, due to its location on both the Pacific coast and the international border, Washington attracted more than its share of shady characters, no-good varmints, and others living outside the law.

Smugglers and rumrunners liked Washington because they could easily sneak their goods across the border from Canada by either land or sea. Cattle and horse rustlers flocked to the eastern part of the state because its rugged landscape provided many places to hide stolen livestock and offered enough grass to feed the animals. Thieves and murderers indulged themselves in the relative lawlessness of many early Washington boomtowns, and social misfits or those hiding from the law enjoyed the secluded life that could be found in the Cascade Mountains.

But because the state is not readily associated with the Wild West, the outlaws of Washington's early days remain largely unstudied and undocumented. *Outlaw Tales of Washington* uncovers some of these rowdy characters and some of the Evergreen State's most outrageous and interesting crimes.

Lawrence Kelly

In March 1891, Lawrence Kelly snuck onto his four-ton sloop with another illegal batch of opium. The sixty-five half-pound cans he carried would fetch a tidy profit. But only if he was careful. The law had been getting too close to him lately, so he decided to travel a more circuitous route. That day, he sailed from Victoria, British Columbia, to Olympia, Washington. From there, he walked to the train station at Tenino twenty miles away, carrying the opium in a satchel. At Tenino he boarded a southbound train.

Unfortunately for Kelly, U.S. Customs agent Charles Mulkey of Tacoma boarded the same train. While walking through the smoking car, he spotted the bag Kelly was carrying and immediately became suspicious. He walked over, seized it, and began to search it, despite protests from Kelly. When he found the cans of illegal opium, he arrested Kelly. When the train stopped at Castle Rock, Mulkey took Kelly and a nearby witness off the train and headed back to Tacoma, where Kelly appeared before the U.S. commissioner.

How did Lawrence Kelly become a smuggler of opium? His early life showed no signs of defiance; in fact, it seemed just the opposite. Kelly was born about 1839 in the British Isles. When he was a young man, he joined the British Army and then later became a sailor. His British sloop docked at New Orleans just after the American Civil War broke out, so he deserted the ship and joined the Confederate Army.

Shortly after the end of war, Kelly immigrated west, sailing around South America on the ship *Young America* and ending up in the Pacific Northwest. His life of crime began about 1872, when he was caught smuggling Canadian silks into the United States. He was fined $500, but this punishment didn't curb his smuggling. His smuggling operation soon made him enough money to build a nice home on Guemes Island, just across Guemes Channel from Anacortes. His house stood high on a bluff, from which Kelly had an awe-inspiring view of the Guemes Channel, Bellingham Channel, and Rosario Strait.

In 1877, he married Lizzie Coutts, almost twenty years his junior. Shortly after their wedding, he transferred the title of his house to his wife, so that if he was ever arrested, the house could not be seized to pay his fines. This act seems to indicate he never planned to make a living by legitimate means. For a time, he and Lizzie easily lived off the money he made as a smuggler.

At first Kelly used an ordinary fishing sloop to carry illegal goods from Canada to Washington state. His bright red boat was easily visible, but the authorities didn't bother him. He could outrun the law anyway. He knew all the coves and bays like the back of his hand, and his small boat could travel easily in shallow water through which the bigger customs boats couldn't pass. He smeared pot black and tallow on his boat to make it glide more easily through the water. If someone chased him and he couldn't get away, he dumped the smuggled goods overboard so he wouldn't be caught with them.

Smuggling was not an unheard-of crime in the United States in the nineteenth century. During the Civil War, liquor, blankets, and wool were smuggled from Canada into the United States for use by soldiers. Smuggling increased dramatically, however, when the railroads began to import large numbers of

Chinese workers as laborers for canneries, hop fields, mines, and public works. Though they caused some difficulties with white workers, Chinese laborers worked hard, took fewer breaks, could be paid less, and did not drink.

Then the Exclusion Act of 1882 prevented Chinese laborers from entering the United States legally. Smugglers saw an opportunity in the Pacific ocean channels between Washington state and British Columbia. In no time at all smugglers began to sneak Chinese workers into the United States, and Kelly joined their ranks. The smugglers took Chinese immigrants to places where a large number of Chinese were already living, so they would blend into the population. Sometimes the smugglers hid the immigrants in the smaller San Juan Islands to wait for the perfect opportunity to take them to the United States mainland. Smugglers generally received $50 per person brought into the country, so smuggling was a good moneymaking operation.

Chinese workers used a large amount of opium, and soon the illegal trade of that commodity grew, too. A refinery in Victoria on Vancouver Island manufactured as much opium as the Chinese workers could ever want. Opium could be imported legally, but it was very highly taxed, so the drug was often smuggled into the country to avoid the customs duty.

Whether his cargo was human or other contraband, it made no difference to Kelly. He would smuggle anything. But once his activities were discovered, the law was perpetually at his heels.

Customs agent Thomas Caine noticed that Kelly frequently used the Swinomish Channel, between Fidalgo Island and the mainland, to deliver his stolen goods. On December 21, 1882, Caine hid in the Channel, waiting for Kelly to show up.

For some reason Kelly suspected he was being watched. As he approached the area where Caine hid, he quietly jumped into the water and swam, pushing his boat in front of him. In spite of Kelly's stealth, Caine could still see the boat when it appeared out of the early morning fog. He waited until the sloop got close, then ordered Kelly to surrender. Kelly did, without a fight. He was carrying forty cases of Chinese wine and a man from China, both illegal. Fortunately for Kelly, the Chinese man testified at Kelly's hearing that he was not a "coolie," or illegal Chinese immigrant, but a merchant with business in Portland. Kelly was cleared of the smuggling charge but was fined $150 for the illegal importation of Chinese wine.

The incident did nothing to deter Kelly. In July of 1883, the authorities caught Kelly with illegal goods and fined him $390. Four months later, on November 17, he was assessed a fine of $20. The fines were just minor annoyances to Kelly.

In 1886, he bought some property on Sinclair Island from Thomas P. Hogin, also registering this property in his wife's name. From high on a bluff, the house had a commanding view of the waterways. He could see the Strait of Georgia that ran between Washington state and Vancouver Island. From this vantage point, he could easily watch for customs ships.

By outward appearances, Kelly seemed to be living an ordinary life. He and his wife had six children who attended school on Sinclair Island. At one time, Kelly was a member of the school board. If the townspeople were aware of his occupation, they didn't harass him about it. Perhaps some even sympathized with him. By the late 1880s, he mainly smuggled opium from Victoria. He stashed the opium on Vancouver Island until the weather was favorable and a successful delivery on the mainland was likely. Then he took the opium to Port Townsend, Seattle, or some other Washington port. He made about $12 per pound of the drug.

Not long after moving to Sinclair Island, Kelly had another serious brush with the law. Customs inspectors seized his Whitehall boat on May 16, 1886, in Tacoma. Unfortunately for Kelly, he had just loaded 567 tins of opium, equivalent to 364 pounds. He was held on a bail of $3,000. In the end, Kelly was fined only $100, but the seizure of his boat threatened to end his career.

But his luck had not yet run out. In fact, he got right back into the business and seemed to work with impunity. Dozens of his deliveries around the Puget Sound area went undetected, even though the customs boats were getting stronger and faster, and smugglers were getting caught more and more frequently. Kelly and others devised new tricks to keep from getting arrested. Kelly put the opium in a weighted sack, tied the sack to a rope, and tied the rope to a ring bolted into the hull of his boat. The boat dragged the opium along underwater, so that a casual inspection of the ship would detect nothing on deck. Sometimes Kelly tied a sack of opium to a float when customs inspectors came near, and then he would retrieve it when the inspectors were gone.

The smuggling of Chinese immigrants became more dangerous too. To hide them, some smugglers resorted to sewing them into potato sacks, then stashing them in some small cubbyhole of the ship. Anyone who inspected the ship might conclude the ship was transporting a cargo of vegetables. Sometimes the Chinese were left on an uninhabited island or on barren rocks to wait for a boat to take them to the mainland. Supposedly smugglers even tossed the illegal immigrants overboard in order to avoid arrest. Kelly always denied doing that, but he admitted that sometimes he delivered the Chinese back to Vancouver Island and let them believe they were in the United States.

Herbert Foote Beecher, son of the famous evangelist Reverend Henry Ward Beecher, came to Washington in 1883. For two years he plied the waters between Port Townsend and the San Juan Islands in his gospel ship Evangel. He heard stories about Kelly and other smugglers, and it wasn't long before the information he obtained led to arrests, larger fines, and confiscation of greater amounts of opium. Kelly was captured several times and paid increasingly higher fines.

Efforts like Beecher's led to Kelly's 1891 arrest by customs agent Mulkey aboard the train. When he appeared before the U.S. commissioner in Tacoma, Kelly denied ownership of the satchel. He claimed that Mulkey planted the opium in his bag while he was in the washroom. The commissioner did not believe him and sentenced him to two years at the McNeil Island Federal Penitentiary. Amazingly, Kelly's neighbors on Sinclair Island did believe him. They tried to petition for Kelly's release, but they were unsuccessful.

Customs officers converged on Kelly's hideout at Sinclair Island. They took his ship Alert and sold it for $3,221.83 to pay his fines. They couldn't prove he had transported illegal opium, but they could at least charge him with entering and leaving foreign ports without proper paperwork. They claimed he had been to Victoria and back several times without declaring his manifest.

While he was at McNeil Island, Kelly's fines mounted to the point where he had to sell his island property in order to pay them. To support herself, his wife kept house for a man in Anacortes whose wife was hospitalized. After his release, Kelly went to Anacortes in a drunken rage and threatened his wife with a gun. She alerted the police, but Kelly had disappeared.

In 1896 Kelly stole a box of tools from carpenter D. J. Davis of Anacortes. A man named J. H. Young became suspicious when he saw Kelly and another man sneaking toward the wharf, so Young asked Davis to check on his tools. They were missing, so Young, Davis, and J. A. Crookham formed a search party. Marshal Stevenson, J. W. Bird, H. H. Soufle, R. McCormick, and George Layton formed another.

At first neither search party could find the two men, but then Young spotted Kelly in a boat off Guemes Island. The marshal's party followed the Fidalgo Island shore and circled around Burrows Bay. Young's party sailed across the bay to Cypress Island, where they found two men and their camp but no boat or tool chest. Somehow Kelly slipped away again. The next day the marshal went back to the island to resume the search. He found a cabin and a dog. Stevenson, Bird, and Soufle snuck up to the cabin and peered inside. There they found Kelly asleep, so they pounded on the door and demanded entrance. Kelly opened the door, and he was immediately arrested. He resisted briefly, but when he tried to get to his rifle, Stevenson knocked him down and handcuffed him.

The posse returned to Anacortes. While their boat docked, Kelly jumped overboard and disappeared into the water. He somehow swam away, even though he was handcuffed. A week later a man named Ipsen spotted two men and a boat on the beach near Deception Pass between Fidalgo Island and Whidbey Island. He watched them for a short time and became

Lawrence Kelly, testifying at Port Townsend, circa 1900.
(From the Collection of the Jefferson County Historical Society, Port Townsend, Washington)

convinced they were smugglers. He disguised himself as a settler and approached their camp. By the time he arrived the men were gone, but a search of their tent yielded about $5,000 worth of opium. Ipsen suspected the stash belonged to Lawrence Kelly, but others didn't think so. They figured that Kelly knew the Puget Sound area too well to let himself be trapped on an island by a high tide.

The next day one hundred feet of cable was stolen from a local sloop, five boxes of codfish were taken from Matheson's wharf, and a rowboat was stolen from W. Mathews's landing on Guemes Island. Because Kelly was known to be in debt due to his fines, he was suspected of the thefts, but no proof of his guilt ever surfaced.

In 1901 Kelly was captured in Seattle. He had just arrived from Vancouver Island and had booked a room at the Granville Hotel. He left two suitcases full of opium in his room while he went out for the evening. Unfortunately he got drunk that night and was picked up by the police. While he was in jail, the Seattle police received a tip from Vancouver Island police. They sent an investigator to Kelly's hotel room, where they found the opium. Amazingly, he paid only a $5 fine, and the opium was not even confiscated.

The next day a Seattle policeman followed Kelly when he left for New Westminster on Vancouver Island. Kelly checked in at the Fraser House, went out for dinner and a stroll, and then returned to the hotel. Once Kelly returned to the hotel, the officer decided he could probably take a break. But that was just what Kelly was counting on. That night, he snuck out and crossed back into Washington. A few months later, as he debarked a steamer in Portland, he was arrested for possession of $800 worth of opium. He spent several months in the Mult-nomah County jail in Oregon.

Kelly appeared in the news again in January 1904, when customs agent Fred F. Strickling heard that Kelly was going to try to smuggle opium by train. He boarded the train at its northern-most stop in Washington at Sumas, near the Canadian border. He figured he would have no trouble intercepting Kelly. At each train stop, he asked the conductor if anyone had boarded. Finally, the conductor answered in the affirmative: A man boarded the train at Nooksack.

Strickling strode down the aisle until he found the man the conductor had described. He approached the man and told him he needed to look inside his valise. Kelly was defiant and refused. When Strickling insisted, Kelly shoved him out of the way and fled down the aisle. Before Strickling could react, Kelly jumped off the train. Strickling pulled the emergency cord, and the train stopped. Inside Kelly's luggage were sixty-five tins of opium. Strickling ordered the engineer to back up the train to the place at which Kelly had jumped off.

Luckily for Strickling, Kelly knocked himself out when he jumped. Strickling quickly handcuffed him, confiscated his gun, and took him on the train to Deming. Kelly's face and shoulders were cut up from his rough landing in the cinders along the track, so the Deming station agent asked a local doctor to patch up the prisoner. Shortly afterward, Strickling escorted Kelly to Sumas and on to Bellingham, where he was arraigned before U.S. Commissioner H. B. Williams. He was released for $1,000 in bail, after which posting, he promptly skipped town.

He was at large for over a year, until Fred E. King and Fred C. Dean captured Kelly on July 18, 1905, near Anderson

Island. They had disguised themselves as fishermen trolling the areas of Puget Sound that Kelly was known to haunt. They pretended to be just passing by, when they approached Kelly and pulled out their badges. He surrendered without a fight. He was carrying sixty pounds of opium at the time. He received a two-year sentence at McNeil Island but was released early for good behavior. The moment he was released, a U.S. marshal hauled him straight back to jail in Seattle for the earlier offense on which he had jumped bail. In May 1909, Kelly was sent back to McNeil Island for a one-year sentence.

After his release, Kelly found that going straight meant hard times. He "retired" from his life of crime in 1911, when he was about seventy years old. He contacted the Daughters of the Confederacy and was admitted to a Confederate soldiers' home in Louisiana, where he died. So ended the twenty-five-year career of one of the most notorious smugglers on the Pacific Coast.

The Roslyn Bank Robbery

In 1886 Matt Warner, born Ras Christiansen, then known as Ras Lewis, bought a remote ranch in the grasslands of central Washington, near the future town of Ephrata. Warner intended to use the 7U Ranch as the base of operations for his outlaw gang. His partners in crime included brothers Bill, Tom, and George McCarty, and Bill's son Fred McCarty. All five men had committed crimes of one kind or another throughout the Rocky Mountain states over the past several years. They had moved their operations west to evade the law.

For more than six years the five men terrorized the Northwest, robbing banks in Oregon and hiding out at the Washington ranch. But by the fall of 1892, Warner had had enough and decided to call it quits. His wife and daughter also lived at the ranch, and he knew he was putting their lives in danger. He intended to start a new life as a cattle rancher. But he couldn't resist one more heist. When George McCarty suggested robbing the Benjamin E. Snipes and Company bank in Roslyn, Washington, Warner thought seriously about the scheme. He already had more than $30,000 from previous bank robberies, but that might not be enough to start his cattle ranch. So he went along with McCarty's plan, over the objections of his wife.

At that time, Roslyn was a small town experiencing a big boom caused by the nearby coal mines. McCarty planned to rob the bank shortly after the miner's payroll—an estimated $100,000—was delivered to the bank. McCarty visited the bank and memorized its floor plan. He scouted the area around the bank. Heavy timber surrounded the town, so he figured it would be hard for a posse to chase them. McCarty also found a remote cabin they could use to hide and rest. Afterward, the robbers would take off in different directions to confuse any pursuers. They would meet later at George McCarty's ranch in east-central Oregon.

At one o'clock in the afternoon on September 24, 1892, Warner's gang approached the Roslyn bank. While George and Tom McCarty kept watch outside, Matt Warner and Bill and Fred McCarty strode confidently into the bank and walked directly into the enclosure where the tellers worked. One of the robbers approached a cashier named T. B. Abernathy and demanded that he turn over all the money. Abernathy resisted, so Warner knocked him out with his own gun. Bill and Fred held the other tellers and some customers at gunpoint as Warner stuffed several canvas bags full of money from an open safe.

While the robbery was in progress, some miners approached the bank to collect their pay, but Tom and George McCarty kept them away by firing at them. The assistant cashier, F. A. Frasier, arrived at the bank and saw what was happening. He ran to a nearby hardware store and quickly recruited some men and procured some weapons. The men were on guard as they approached the robbers outside the bank. George and Tom McCarty turned their fire on them. In a brief skirmish, Frasier was wounded in the hip and another man was shot in the leg. The rest of the men backed off.

Just then, Warner and Bill and Fred McCarty ran outside with the loot. The five men mounted their horses and rode hard toward the timber north of town. A posse led by L. R. Thomas soon followed the bank robbers. About twelve miles east of town, three of the outlaws and some members of the posse unexpectedly ran into each other. Both sides were startled, and a moment or two passed before the groups realized they should fire on each other. Amazingly, the bandits survived the close call and escaped.

The robbers rode for the cabin that George McCarty had previously located. There they rested for a while and divided the money. Reports differ widely on exactly how much money was stolen from the bank. In his autobiography, Warner claimed the booty amounted to about $30,000, but contemporary newspapers reported much less than that—between $5,000 and $10,000. This was because the expected miners' payroll had not yet been delivered from the company office. Once the money was split, each robber headed in a different direction, expecting to meet at Bill McCarty's ranch at a later date. Warner acted as if he were going along with the plan but, in fact, he rode north toward the 7U Ranch to pick up his wife and daughter.

The next day, Warner spotted a posse riding toward him along the Columbia River. Tall basalt cliffs stood behind him, and the mighty river flowed in front of him. He couldn't scale the cliffs, so he had to take his chances with the river. He threw off everything except his money belt. Then he spurred his horse into the water.

The river was swift and high and full of tricky whirlpools and undercurrents. Battling the raging waterway was a terrible risk for Warner to take, but he figured death by drowning was better than facing the gallows. Warner struggled to stay on his horse while it gallantly swam the swift current. When the officers onshore started firing at him, Warner fought to stay afloat while keeping his head out of sight of the officers. Finally his horse was pushed toward the opposite bank by the current, and man and animal stumbled ashore. Safe at last, Warner collapsed for a two-hour rest before riding on to the 7U Ranch.

Some doubts exist about whether this incident actually happened as reported in Warner's autobiography; contemporary papers did not report the event at all. In fact, the generally accepted story is that the posse searched for several days and never encountered the robbers. Apparently they found only three hard-ridden horses that were left behind by the outlaws. After the return of the posse, Abernathy posted a $1,000 reward for the capture of the bandits. Mr. Abrams, manager of an Ellensburg bank, added another $1,000, and Governor Terry added $500 to the pot.

Posses searched all over Washington and Oregon for the bandits and picked up anybody who looked suspicious. Bank owner Ben Snipes also hired Spokane detective M. C. Sullivan to hunt for them in eastern Oregon. Sullivan arrested three men named Cal Hale, Tom Kimzie, and George Zachary and took them to the county seat at Ellensburg for trial. A preliminary hearing was held on November 30. Several witnesses agreed that the three men were the ones who had robbed the bank, and a trial was set for January 3, 1893. Snipes hired renowned attorney H. J. Snively to assist the newly elected prosecuting attorney E. E. Wager.

The trial was delayed twenty-seven days when one of the state's key witnesses became ill, but finally each of the three men was tried separately. Hale was the first to be tried. Eyewitnesses Frazier, Abernathy, and George Jenkins, principal of Roslyn schools, identified Hale as one of the men present in the bank that day. The postmaster of Hale's hometown testified that it would have been impossible for Hale to have participated in the bank robbery as he had visited the post office that day to mail a letter. The postmark on the letter proved his statement. Hale was convicted anyway and given a prison sentence. Both Zachary and Kimzie were released after their juries voted for acquittal. Hale was also later released from jail.

Snipes fumed both at the delay in the trial and the subsequent release of the suspects. He couldn't understand how the perpetrators could be released. Then prosecutor Wager received an interesting letter written by Sarah Morgan, of Salt Lake City, Utah, who claimed to know exactly who the Roslyn bank bandits were. She provided names and dates that were hard to doubt. She declared she was telling what she knew because Tom McCarty had jilted her in favor of another woman. She was also upset with Warner for marrying her younger sister. At the same time she was fearful that McCarty would come after her for telling on them, so she requested that Wager provide protection for her until his conviction.

Meanwhile, Warner reached the 7U Ranch. He had intended to leave the state, but his wife was pregnant. Now they would have to stay at the ranch until the baby was born, which was December 30, 1892. Shortly afterward, he read in the newspaper that men had gone to Utah to gather information about the case. He knew his sister-in-law had blown his cover. He had to make tracks fast.

But he was too late. On April 1, 1893, five men posing as miners rode up to his cabin and asked for breakfast. They were actually deputized officers led by City Marshal P. C. McGrath of Ellensburg. The other men were Dick Hart, Harvey Skillman, Billy Wallace, and Charles Wallace. The men subdued

Warner after a struggle. They took him to the Ellensburg jail. McGrath had also captured George McCarty in Oregon and brought him back for trial.

The consequences looked grim for Warner and McCarty. They started hatching a plot to escape from jail. Another jailbird advised them to get a lawyer, which they did. A man named Johns agreed to represent them at the preliminary hearing that would be held on April 24. He claimed he could get them off if they had enough money for payoffs. Warner had more than $40,000 buried on his property, but he didn't know if he could trust the lawyer with it. But if he didn't, he might not get the chance to spend it himself anyway. Reluctantly, he drew Johns a map to show him how to find the money.

Sarah Morgan testified at the preliminary hearing. She said she had overheard her brother-in-law talk about robbing a bank and later heard him mention the Roslyn bank specifically. J. M. McDonald testified that the suspect named George McCarty was the man he had seen holding the horses in front of the bank. Warner was held on $10,000 bail; McCarty's bail was set at $7,000. The judge had decided there was enough evidence to hold the two men for trial.

Warner and McCarty were shocked that they would be standing trial. They had thought the bribes had guaranteed there would be no trial. From then on they spent all their waking moments planning a jailbreak. Two weeks before the trial, they paid another inmate to smuggle them some tools and weapons. For several days they sawed through the jail bars to their cell door. Finally, one Saturday night, they severed the bars enough to squeeze out the cell door into a hallway. Several windows along that hallway opened onto the street at ground level. They used a crowbar to pry out the bricks around one of the windows, an activity that took most of the night.

At daylight, they made their break. Grabbing some guns that had been hidden for them under the sidewalk, they slipped out of the Ellensburg jail. They thought the streets might be empty on a Sunday morning, but they were wrong. Two men named Ed Grady and Mose Bollman spotted them running from the jail and fired at them. McCarty fired back, striking Bollman in the wrist. The outlaws dashed into the nearby home of J. C. Clymer, where Clymer's wife and son were at home. They told them as long as they kept quiet they wouldn't be hurt.

In a short time, Marshal McGrath and a gang of men gathered outside the Clymer home. Warner allowed McGrath to come inside. He told the marshal that he would go back to the jail if he would clear the crowd away. He didn't want to have to shoot anybody. McGrath agreed, and he walked the two prisoners back to the jail. Despite the escape attempt, the trial ended with a hung jury. Amazingly, only four jurors voted for Warner's conviction; eight voted for his acquittal. The vote was five for conviction and seven for acquittal for McCarty. The judge ordered a new trial to be held on July 24, 1893, but the prosecuting attorney suddenly moved to dismiss the case because of lack of evidence. Of course this wasn't really true— Warner's payoff money had simply finally reached the pockets of the prosecutor. According to Warner's autobiography, his attorney had discovered that the prosecuting attorney had a relationship with the chief witness, Sarah Morgan. To keep the scandal quiet, the prosecutor had agreed to recommend dismissal of the case. All of Warner's money had been used to accomplish this. To show he wasn't completely unscrupulous, the lawyer returned $500 to Warner.

As soon as they left the jail, McCarty and Warner went their separate ways. Warner went to Diamond Mountain, Utah, where he had once been part of a rustling operation. But this time he planned to stay "legit," and he made that intention known to all his old outlaw friends. One day he ran into his father-in-law at a general store. The man helped Warner get in touch with his wife, Rose, who was then living in Boise, Idaho. After a brief correspondence, Rose rejoined her husband in Utah.

Warner took a job as a guard for a miner who was moving his operation to the Diamond Mountains and wanted to protect his equipment. While they moved the equipment, they were ambushed by thieves. Two of the attackers were killed; a third was injured. Despite eyewitnesses who claimed Warner had acted in self-defense, Warner was arrested for murder. The judge in the trial was not sympathetic due to Matt Warner's past life of crime. He sentenced Warner to five years in the Utah State Penitentiary. Warner moved to Price, Utah, after serving three years and four months of his sentence.

Several years later he was appointed deputy sheriff there. Rose had died a few years earlier, so Warner remarried and had three more children. He died on December 21, 1938.

As far as the McCarty family is concerned, Bill and Fred were killed while holding up the Farmers and Merchants Bank in Delta, Colorado, on September 7, 1893. Tom escaped that incident and fled to Montana, where he disappeared into obscurity. Where George went after the trial in Ellensburg is not known.

The legend of the bank robbery lived on for quite some time. Afterward, many people in Roslyn buried their money rather than entrust it to a bank. One miner died before he could tell his wife where he had hidden his money. Years later his grown sons found the money in a can under the house. It was badly rotted but usable.

Johnny Schnarr

Johnny Schnarr checked his supplies one last time. His boat was in tip-top shape, and the typical winter storms had not yet touched the region. A few minutes later, Schnarr and his partner, Harry, motored away from the dock at Victoria, British Columbia. Their destination was San Francisco. Their cargo was prime Canadian rum. November 8, 1920, was off to a promising start.

Schnarr set a course through the Strait of Juan de Fuca between Washington State and Canada and out to the Pacific Ocean. He picked up his contraband at Pedder Bay at the southern tip of Vancouver Island then headed for the open sea. The operation seemed to be going so well, he decided to risk a little catnap. He had been up for almost twenty-four hours straight and was exhausted. He left Harry at the helm.

Two hours later, Schnarr awoke from his nap. Harry was struggling with the wheel. Schnarr pushed him out of the way and attempted to gain control of the boat. Once he had the boat stabilized, he got his bearings. He was astounded—somehow Harry had turned the boat nearly 180 degrees heading back toward the port of origin! In a chastened voice, Harry admitted he really didn't know that much about boating.

Schnarr cursed Harry and put the boat back on course. He got them around Cape Flattery, the northwestern tip of Washington, before the motor began to cough and sputter. Schnarr fixed the problem, but the boat was using so much gas and oil that he knew they would not have enough fuel to get all the way to San Francisco.

They stopped at Astoria, on the mouth of the Columbia River, to stock up on fuel. But their bad luck continued when they left town. The tide was out, and they ran aground on a sandbar. They had to wait six hours before the tide came in to float them off the sand.

They made good progress for the next two days. Schnarr set the course and hoped nothing else would go wrong. He decided to risk taking another nap, despite the unreliable Harry. Once again, he couldn't hold the course. The boat ran aground again, and the resulting crunch woke Schnarr from his sleep. The treacherous waves threatened to pound the stranded boat to bits. The men had no choice but to abandon ship. They struggled through the waves and collapsed on the shore. Once he was rested, Schnarr realized that some of the cargo might be saved. Between waves, Schnarr waded back to the marooned boat. He opened the hatch cover and pulled out a sack of liquor. When the next big wave receded, he made a break for the beach. He dropped the sack to the sand and rested a minute before going after another load. Eventually Schnarr and Harry recovered seventy of the 110 cases of liquor before the boat was completely broken up by the waves.

Schnarr's career as a rumrunner was not off to a very good start. But he had not chosen this career on purpose. It had happened by accident.

Johnny Schnarr began his life on November 16, 1894, in the small town of Chehalis, Washington. He had two older brothers, August and Gus, and a younger sister, Minnie. When he was six years old, the family moved to a twenty-six-acre plot on Coal Creek, three miles from Chehalis. When he was eleven, the Brown Logging Company wanted to build a railway through the county, and the Schnarr property lay right in its path. In exchange for their property, the railroad built the Schnarrs a new log house in another location.

In 1910, Johnny's older brothers went to work at a logging camp on Cracroft Island, about 150 miles west of Vancouver Island, British Columbia. The next Spring young Johnny joined them. After logging operations finished in the fall, the brothers looked around for trapping prospects. They camped on the east side of Vancouver Island and spent the winter there. Here Schnarr developed skills he would one day use in his future career. In addition to all he learned about trapping, he also learned a lot about sailing, weather, and the sea. He even learned to make dugout canoes from watching the Indians.

The following summer the boys got hand logging rights for an area on the Adams River in British Columbia. In the fall and winter they made a living by trapping. The next summer, the Schnarr brothers worked in a logging camp and again spent the winter trapping.

The following spring, the Schnarr brothers tried their hands at fishing on the Klinaklini River in British Columbia. There, Johnny Schnarr met his future employer, Fred Kohse. Out fishing one day, the Schnarr brothers helped Kohse get his small rowboat unstuck from a gravel bar. To thank them, he gave them a ride in his sailboat, which was anchored at the mouth of the river. When they got to Victoria, Kohse offered them jobs at his boathouse. August and Johnny Schnarr accepted; Gus Schnarr returned to Chehalis. While working for Kohse, Schnarr learned a lot about fixing engines and navigating a boat on the ocean.

Schnarr took a five-year hiatus from fishing and logging to serve his country in World War I, but he returned to his home state after the armistice. He resumed his life as a logger near

Hoquiam on Gray's Harbor on the Washington coast. While there, he received a letter from Kohse, who asked if he would be willing to run a boatload of liquor for a friend named Harry. Harry needed someone good with engines.

In Victoria, Kohse introduced Schnarr to Harry. Harry offered Schnarr $500 to drive his boat to San Francisco and back. Schnarr would be the ship's mechanic, navigator, and rumrunner. The Volstead Act of 1919 had made it illegal to import liquor into the United States, but Johnny Schnarr accepted Harry's offer anyway. The boat turned out to be a little smaller than Schnarr would have liked, but he had already accepted the job. As it turned out, he had reason to be wary; his partner proved completely unskilled.

After Schnarr and Harry wrecked off the Oregon Coast, they stashed their liquor on the beach then walked north to what was probably the Cape Blanco lighthouse. They were stuck in Oregon with no money and no way home. Finally Harry's girlfriend sent cash to pay their return fare. Kohse paid Schnarr $100, despite the fact that he had not been able to deliver the cargo. Then they parted ways.

Schnarr returned to Chehalis and resumed his logging job, but in March of 1921 he received another letter from Kohse. He wanted Schnarr to run liquor from Canada into Washington state. He would split the profit three ways between Schnarr, himself, and his partner, Billy Garraro. The boat he would use was eighteen feet long and had a one-cylinder, five-horsepower engine. Its top speed was five knots. Schnarr liked the terms and accepted the offer.

His first delivery was to Anacortes, Washington, on the northern tip of Fidalgo Island. His customer was Consolidated

Exporters, located about five miles north of downtown. The company would become one of Schnarr's top customers. The boat he used was in top shape, and he no longer had to deal with an unreliable shipmate. Schnarr's only worry was the United States Coast Guard cutter Arcata, which had a top speed of twelve knots and carried a cannon with a range of 4,000 yards. Although the Arcata was faster than Schnarr's boat, it generally patrolled much farther south. For a while, Schnarr made his runs undisturbed.

In the first month, he made more than $1,000 in just five or six trips. He and Garraro picked up the booze in Victoria, then they sped toward their destination, taking turns steering so they didn't get tired. When they came within a certain distance of the shoreline, Schnarr stopped the boat. Then he exchanged flashlight signals with his customers waiting onshore. If he received the appropriate signal in return, he would drop a skiff in the water to haul the liquor to shore. Schnarr usually stayed with the getaway boat, while Garraro rowed the booze to shore and collected the money.

At first, Schnarr carried about seventy-five cases of booze on each trip, but demand was great. Kohse bought a new boat big enough to haul 110 cases at a time. The boat was faster, too—too fast for the Coast Guard to catch. But just in case, Kohse and Schnarr changed their method of operation just a bit. Instead of picking up the booze directly from the supplier in Victoria, Schnarr motored out to Discovery Island, a small island in Haro Strait, and picked up his liquor there.

Conducting business this way was less obvious to the authorities. But an additional hazard developed. Some men, too lazy or too stupid to mess with the business end of rum-running, waited until other rumrunners were already in the process of making their runs. They stole the liquor at gunpoint and sold it to the nearest customer. Mickey, Happy, and Ted Eggers were the most notorious of these pirates. Schnarr kept a wary eye out for these type of men.

Kohse started demanding a bigger percentage of the profits, but Schnarr thought that arrangement was unfair since he was taking all the risks. He severed his relationship with Kohse, and Billy Garraro left with him. Schnarr took a break from rum-running to work on a boat he had designed himself. He hired a Japanese carpenter and shipbuilder to build the boat to his specifications and borrowed money to buy an engine for the boat. He found a powerful six-cylinder, eighty-horsepower Marmon car engine. He spent about three weeks installing it on the boat, which he called Moonbeam. Its top speed was seventeen or eighteen knots, and it was able to carry about seventy-five cases of liquor.

In the fall of 1923, the boat was ready to go. Autumn was the perfect time to get started. Schnarr generally avoided making deliveries in the summer because the nights were too short. He needed to be able to make the round-trip to and from the delivery point under cover of darkness. Ready for a busy season with a new boat, he already had several customers lined up. Some of them were men he had met while working for Kohse.

The first of these were brothers-in-law Carl Melby and Pete Peterson. They supplied liquor to the greater Seattle area, using a Cadillac and a Studebaker to carry their liquor loads. The cars had heavy-duty springs so the weight they were carrying would not be noticeable. To confuse the authorities, Schnarr used different drop-off locations every time he delivered to Melby and Peterson. He delivered liquor to ports all over Puget Sound, from Port Angeles to Anacortes. Unfortunately the lucrative relationship was threatened when Schnarr noticed that Peterson was shorting him. He threatened to end their association unless Melby handled all the money. After looking into the situation, Melby noticed that he had been shorted too. He put an end to those shenanigans, and the liquor deliveries continued.

One time Schnarr made a run to a small bay about a mile east of Port Angeles. By the time he arrived, a strong wind had risen, causing twenty-foot waves. His contact, Barney Sampson, suggested that they tie up at the government wharf in Port Angeles to wait out the storm. Schnarr agreed, not wanting to test his luck twice in one night. Schnarr was astonished when the harbormaster told him that the Coast Guard cutter Arcata was tied up on the other side. Before the sun came up the next morning, Schnarr left the harbor before he got caught.

Run-ins with the law weren't the only hazards of Schnarr's trade. He was equally cautious of submerged logs and debris. Puget Sound was always full of them due to the region's logging activity and storms. More than once Schnarr's boat suffered damage from logs he couldn't see until he had run into them. He also had to be wary of fog, which could roll in thick and fast. Schnarr knew Puget Sound so well that he was usually able to reach his destination despite fog, but one time he sheared most of the blades off both propellers when his boat cruised over submerged rocks. He limped back to port at about three knots with only one blade left. On another trip he almost collided with an ocean liner hidden by the fog, but managed to avoid it in the nick of time.

In 1923 a new man came to Seattle to enforce Prohibition. He was a tough ex-cattleman from Wyoming named Carl Jackson. He immediately hired more men to patrol the wharves. Schnarr had to be more careful about where he dropped off his liquor.

His friends in the local police force usually tipped him off when there was going to be a raid, but he did have a close call or two. One night, just as Garraro reached the beach with his skiff full of thirty cases of booze, Prohibition agents popped out of the forest. Fortunately, the raid didn't seem very organized, and Garraro, Melby, and Peterson were able to split up. They raced through the trees on foot while Schnarr watched helplessly from his position offshore in the Moonbeam. Fortunately, the men escaped, though Jackson was shot in the sole of his foot.

Another close call came later that winter. The Shore Patrol caught Schnarr's team near Deception Pass on the north end of Whidbey Island. Just as they were about to offload their cargo into the rowboat, lights came on and the Shore Patrol started blasting away. In his haste to escape the spray of bullets, Garraro cut off the anchor rather than haul it in. Once again, the smugglers avoided detection. Or so Schnarr thought. The next day a customs inspector came around the Victoria docks and found a lead bullet lodged in the hull of the *Moonbeam* and knew what had happened. Rather than argue the case, Schnarr paid the man the $500 fee. He didn't want to be out of commission too long, or he'd be out much more than that in lost profits.

In the spring of 1924, a new threat arrived in the waters. The U.S. Customs Service launched ten new boats in the Puget Sound area. Their top speed was about eighteen knots, the same speed as Schnarr's own boat. He knew he'd need a new engine. This time he bought one that he figured wouldn't have to be replaced for quite a while. With a three-hundred-horse-power Fiat airplane engine with a top speed of thirty knots, he would easily outrun the Coast Guard and the Customs Service. He adapted the airplane engine for use on the boat, but he couldn't change the fact that this type of engine had no gears. That meant it had no reverse, so he would have to be sure he was pointing the boat in the right direction before starting it.

For the next two years, Schnarr had a steady job running rum into Washington. He ran booze all year except during the longest days of summer. Soon he realized that he needed a bigger boat. He could only carry seventy-five cases, and many customers wanted one hundred or more at a time. He designed a new boat forty-eight feet long with a nine-foot beam. Luckily, the new boat's construction was already in the works when some friends borrowed the old boat to make a run and lost it when the Coast Guard shot it up then forced it into a crash landing on a beach. The friends escaped unhurt, but Schnarr's own rum-running business was out of commission for a month while he put the finishing touches on his new boat. Schnarr took the rare opportunity for a little leisure. He spent some of his spare time at the horse races at Willow's Fairgrounds and Race Track, where he met his first wife. He married Pearl Bromely in December 1927 in Tacoma. Pearl had a daughter named Doreen by a previous marriage, and two years later the couple would have a son named Johnny. Eventually they bought a house on Vancouver Island, where they frequently treated their friends to hunting and fishing trips.

Meanwhile, Schnarr finished building his new boat, the *Miss Victoria*. This one had two three-hundred-horsepower

Fiat engines, but the design of the cabin proved difficult for loading and unloading cargo. In the fall of 1928, Schnarr built a new boat with a four-hundred-horsepower Liberty airplane engine. Fully loaded with 125 cases, it could still go thirty knots. He called this boat *Miss Victoria II*.

He set off on a trip to deliver to Melby on Dungeness Spit near Sequim on the Olympic Peninsula. Initially the weather was good, with only a light breeze. But when the tide started to come in, huge breakers formed in the shallow areas. Schnarr must not have realized the seriousness of the conditions, because he proceeded with his delivery as normal. As the *Miss Victoria II* approached shore, Schnarr looked for his flashlight signal. When he saw it, he sent his assistant, a man named Griffith, to shore in a flat-bottomed skiff loaded with liquor. As Griffith approached the shore, a big wave caught the small boat and flipped it over, dumping Griffith and the booze. Fortunately, another wave caught Griffith and deposited his unconscious body on the beach. Miraculously, he was unharmed. Even more miraculous, Griffith managed to recover all the liquor. Not even one bottle was broken. After resting, Griffith rowed back out to the *Miss Victoria II*. He was swamped one more time by the waves on his way out, but this time he was ready for it. He climbed aboard the skiff again and reached the *Miss Victoria II* without further incident.

Schnarr used the *Miss Victoria II* for about two years before he needed an even bigger boat. By that time many rumrunners had been caught, but the demand for liquor was just as high as ever. Schnarr figured he could pick up the slack and make two or three deliveries on one trip if he had a bigger boat.

The new boat was forty-five feet long with a ten-foot beam and two four-hundred-horsepower engines. Now he could carry two hundred cases and still reach a speed of thirty knots. He named the new boat *Kitnayakwa* after a river in northern British Columbia. He chose the name because he figured it would be hard for witnesses to remember if he was ever spotted. On one of his first trips in that boat, the Coast Guard tried to run him down. He didn't have any rum onboard, so he could easily go forty knots. The cutters still could go only about seventeen knots, and their cannon fire fell well short of the mark.

One December night Schnarr was delivering some liquor at Discovery Bay, behind the Quimper Peninsula. He didn't spot the Coast Guard cutter until it was about 100 yards away. He quickly got up speed, but the cutter started firing. He couldn't continue on his current course toward a bay or he'd be trapped, so Schnarr quickly turned the boat 180 degrees around and passed within one hundred feet of the cutter. The wash from Schnarr's boat spoiled the sniper's aim just a bit. By the time the bulky cutter turned around, Schnarr was well out of range. Five more cutters were out there waiting to ambush him, but with his superior speed, Schnarr got away easily. The next day he had to repair eighteen bullet holes in the hull of his boat. He lost some of his liquor, but otherwise he was unharmed. Later, he learned that $25,000 had been offered for the capture of his boat.

One time on a stormy night delivery, the boat's engine suddenly died. As Schnarr repaired a plugged gas line, a hose came loose. Gasoline sprayed all over the work area and on Schnarr. As Schnarr struggled to complete the repair, a wrench slipped from his hand and struck an electrical contact. The force was enough to create a spark, and the spilled gas quickly caught on fire—along with Schnarr's arm. Billy Garraro quickly helped put out the fire but not before Schnarr's arm was seriously burned. The boat was not badly damaged, and the two men made their delivery as usual. Though Schnarr later visited a doctor who treated his arm, the incident underscored the danger of his work.

About this time the United States started pressuring Canada to tighten up its shipping laws to prevent the illegal entry of liquor. The new laws meant that liquor could not leave directly from a Canadian port. Rumrunners would have to meet ships out in the ocean to pick up their booze. Schnarr knew his boat wasn't designed for the open ocean, so it was time to build yet another boat. The project would have to wait for a while because Schnarr didn't have the money, but he did his best with the boat he had and used a new rendezvous point one hundred miles out to sea.

Though the swells were larger and the sea rougher farther out, Schnarr made his first few runs without incident. But each trip used much more gas, and the length of each run was doubled. As many as twelve hours were required for each pickup, then another twelve hours were needed for the delivery and return to Victoria. On top of that, two new, fast Canadian cutters patrolled the Strait of Juan de Fuca, and a more ambitious U.S. Coast Guard had stepped up their patrols. Schnarr was nearly caught several times, but he always got away.

At about this time Schnarr discovered that Garraro had cheated him. One of their customers didn't pay them on delivery, so a few days later he sent Garraro to Seattle to collect the money. Garraro returned two days later and told Schnarr the man didn't have the payment. Schnarr figured he'd just have to write off the loss. A couple of months later he ran into the man and asked him about the money. He claimed he had paid Garraro when Garraro had gone to see him. Schnarr confronted Garraro, who admitted he took the money. That was the end of their relationship. After that Tom Colley and Joe Fleming usually accompanied Schnarr on deliveries.

Consolidated Exporters decided they would lend Schnarr the money for a new boat. Schnarr put up $7,000 of his own money, and Consolidated loaned him $15,000 more. Schnarr would pay them 40 percent of every haul to pay off the loan. Business was so good he paid off the debt in less than a year. This boat was fifty-six feet long with two 860-horsepower Packard airplane engines. For added strength, he built the hull with two layers of cedar planks. He christened it *Revuocnav*, another name that would be hard to remember. (It was actually Vancouver spelled backward.) Its top speed was forty knots while fully loaded, but it burned huge amounts of fuel. At a cruising speed of eighteen knots, it used about forty gallons per hour. Schnarr had to carry 2,600 gallons of gas onboard, but he could also carry 250 cases of liquor on this boat.

By this time, Schnarr faced steep competition from other rumrunners, a situation that drove the price of liquor down. He had been getting $11 per case, but now he could get only as much as $5. Sometimes Schnarr's share wouldn't even cover operating costs. But he didn't want to be caught, so he kept running the big gas guzzler.

Once he even took liquor up the Columbia River. He made most of the voyage towed behind a large vessel belonging to Consolidated Exporters. He stayed in international waters, twelve miles off the coast of Washington. When the ship reached the mouth of the Columbia, Schnarr cast himself loose. He hauled four loads of 250 cases each. He offloaded the first two batches before the weather became too risky for a return. Two days later he took the last two loads in. The delivery went off without a hitch.

When Prohibition ended on April 4, 1933, Schnarr's rum-running days were over. In twelve years of full-time rumrunning, Schnarr had made more than four hundred runs for at least ten different buyers and delivered to at least thirty-six different locations in Washington. He delivered at least 60,000 cases of liquor and was never caught. He had about $10,000 in the bank and a nice house. After Prohibition, he sold his boat and went back to logging for a short time. Then he worked as a commercial fisherman up until 1969 when he retired at the age of seventy-five. Out of all the rumrunners, Schnarr may have been the most elusive and the most successful in Washington state.

Thomas Blanck

Frank McMurray was tired of working in the hop fields of North Yakima. He hitched a ride on a train, with no particular destination in mind. While on the train, he met Willie McLaughlin. The two struck up a conversation. McLaughlin told McMurray he was on his way to Tacoma to meet a man named Hamilton. He invited McMurray to join him. They arrived in Tacoma about September 25, 1894.

The two men met Hamilton at a saloon close to the waterfront. For several days, the three men walked around town and made plans to rob a bank. Something didn't sit quite right with McLaughlin so he left town and returned to Yakima.

Hamilton and McMurray continued with their plans. While they walked to a hotel for dinner, Hamilton practiced his quick draw and took pot shots at anything along the way. His skill both impressed and frightened McMurray. He decided that after this robbery he would have nothing more to do with Hamilton.

Both men were right to be wary of Hamilton, known then as Thomas Blanck. His legal name was probably Michael Hogan Jr., though he hadn't used it in years. His criminal history spanned several years in which he committed a string of robberies and murders from Montana to California. He never told McMurray his real name, but let the kid think whatever he wanted.

After dinner they stashed their belongings behind an office. They started to board a train but changed their minds. Blanck and McMurray went to recover their belongings, only to discover someone snooping around. They saw a man take a gun out of their bundle and put it in his pocket. Blanck ran over and demanded that the man give it back.

The man was a Puyallup city marshal named William Jeffery. Jeffery was looking for stolen goods. He saw the two men stash the bundle and wondered if it contained any stolen items. Before Jeffery could respond to Blanck's demand, Blanck pulled out another gun and shot him. Jeffery died instantly. Blanck and McMurray stole a wagon and headed southeast toward Orting. Soon afterward, they split up, hoping to circle back and meet at Palmer farther north.

Meanwhile, Pierce County Sheriff Alexander G. Matthews assembled a posse to hunt for the men who killed Jeffery. Witnesses saw the two men fleeing the scene, and Matthews provided a description to the posse. One man was about five feet nine inches tall and 165 pounds, with a sparse mustache and a tan complexion. He was wearing a black hat, brown coat, striped pants, and new shoes. He looked about twenty-six years old. The other man was about five feet six inches tall with a slender build. He looked much younger, only about eighteen years old. The posse guarded all the main roads, hoping to prevent the murderers' escape.

It didn't take long for the posse to get results. The next day, they captured McMurray at South Prairie, southeast of Tacoma. His hunger was his downfall. He stopped into a cafe to get something to eat. Another diner happened to be a telegraph operator. He thought the man fit the description of a desperado he just read about in a telegraph. He reported the information to the authorities, who picked him up without a struggle.

Blanck proved more elusive. He made it to McMillin, where someone spotted him walking and called out to him. He didn't stop to look before he turned around and fired his gun. Fortunately for Deputy Sheriff Harold Moore, Blanck's shot was wide of its mark. Moore was only slightly injured. Deputies Joseph Welsh and John Ball tended to his wound while Blanck fled.

When they heard about Moore's injury, the posse searched the McMillin area. They hired bloodhound handlers from Ellensburg to give chase. These same dogs tracked bank robbers at Roslyn two years earlier. Unfortunately, there were so many footprints left by the lawmen that the bloodhounds could not pick up the scent. A recent rain also made it difficult for the dogs to track. But the sheriff was confident he had the outlaw surrounded. Matthews hoped that hunger would eventually drive Blanck to seek shelter.

But where was he? He was briefly spotted near Wilkeson, a small town east of Orting. Several men chased him but could not catch him. The lawmen checked out an old Indian cabin that Blanck was supposedly using. But there was no trace of him. Various small clues came in, but none of them amounted to anything.

By the first of October, Blanck had abandoned his original escape route and fled north to Seattle. On October 3, he entered Billy the Mug's Saloon in Seattle about 10:30 p.m. Bartender Charles Bridwell was getting ready to go home. Billy Codrick, owner of the saloon, was counting Bridwell's till when Blanck ran in from the Main Street entrance, waving his gun and yelling. He held a gun on Bridwell and Codrick and told them to stick up their hands. Codrick hoped to distract him by offering him a drink. Instead, Blanck jumped up on the bar and demanded that everyone in the saloon put up their hands. There were about six other people in the bar besides the two employees. Some were playing pool and others were drinking. Ed Spranger tried to sneak out the door, but Blanck saw him and turned his gun on him. Spranger slunk back to his barstool.

Codrick tried to bluff him, telling Blanck that others were coming to the saloon in a short time. Bridwell mentioned that there was a gun in the cash drawer. He started to take the gun from the drawer, when Blanck jumped behind the bar and shot at him. In a fluke, the bullet struck the top of the bar, ricocheted, and went right through Bridwell's heart. Now Blanck had killed two men within the space of a few days.

Blanck jumped back over the bar and fled out the front door. He ran down Main Street and toward the waterfront. Codrick grabbed the gun from the cash drawer and ran after Blanck, but he was already out of sight. He returned to the saloon and called the police.

Officer Gilman T. Philbrick arrived at the saloon almost immediately since he was stationed nearby. Seattle Chief Bolton Rogers and Detectives Edward Cudihee and James L. Wells arrived shortly afterward. They surveyed the saloon and interviewed the witnesses. Blanck was described as five feet nine inches tall and 160 pounds, with a sallow complexion and about four days' growth of beard. He wore a black slouch hat and black sack coat and carried a black gun. As soon as the detectives were through, Coroner Horton took Bridwell's body to the morgue.

Meanwhile, Blanck checked into the Bay View boardinghouse on West and Clay Streets about 11:20 p.m. The next day, he was quietly sitting in his room when Detective Cudihee knocked on his door. Cudihee and Officer John Corbett had tracked him there. They had received a tip from Albert Hartley, whose mother, Amelia Hartley, owned the Bay View house. Hartley had read about the Mug's Saloon shooting and thought the man staying at the house resembled the shooter.

Blanck acted like he didn't suspect anything and let Cudihee into the room. But as soon as he closed the door, he pulled out a gun and aimed it at the detective. Before he had time to think, Cudihee butted the outlaw with his head. The two men struggled over the gun, and Cudihee was grazed in the neck by a stray bullet. Corbett heard the shots and burst into the room. He tried to shoot at Blanck but couldn't risk hitting Cudihee. So he used his weapon to beat Blanck on the head until he let go of Cudihee.

When Blanck fell to the ground, the detectives handcuffed him and took him to jail. He admitted to shooting Bridwell, but claimed it was self-defense. He thought Bridwell was about to shoot him. He was desperate because he had no money. He had only intended to rob the saloon. He denied killing Jeffery, though he admitted knowing about it since he had read the newspapers.

John Scott, the hotel keeper where the Jeffery shooting occurred, visited the jail to identify Blanck. Scott positively identified Blanck as one of the men who had eaten dinner at his hotel. Even though that man had a mustache, Scott felt sure of his identification. Officers found a receipt for a fake beard and mustache in Blanck's room, which would explain his current clean-shaven appearance. The detectives brought McMurray from Tacoma to identify Blanck as the man who killed Jeffery.

McMurray was sure it was him, first by his voice, then his appearance. It was enough evidence to hold Blanck for trial.

Blanck appeared in court on October 5. Judge Joseph M. Glasgow appointed Seattle attorney Gilbert F. Bogue to defend him. He was held without bail. The next day Blanck was arraigned before Judge Thomas J. Humes. Assistant Prosecuting Attorney Austin G. McBride formally charged him with the death of Bridwell. Blanck pled guilty to get it over with. He stated he would rather be executed than go to prison.

His trial began in Seattle on October 16, 1894. It took two days to find an unbiased jury. The prosecutor and the defense delivered their opening remarks. Since Blanck had already pled guilty, the only question for the jury to decide was whether the charge would be first- or second-degree murder. The state would have to prove that the killing of Bridwell was premeditated.

When the coroner testified that Bridwell had died of a gunshot wound, Bogue tried to diffuse the significance of the statement. He argued that the shooting was the result of an accident, that the bullet from a stray gunshot had ricocheted off the bar and hit Bridwell. Blanck had not intended to kill Bridwell. To counter Bogue's testimony, Codrick and Codrick's nephew Edward Reese testified that Blanck was the man who had shot Bridwell. Codrick noted that Blanck had remained calm and collected throughout the time he was in his saloon. He also identified him as the man who threatened him in the saloon.

Other witnesses nailed the lid on Blanck's coffin. Spranger identified him as the man who threatened him in the saloon. Detective Cudihee testified to accosting Blanck in his hotel room and how Blanck had subsequently confessed to having killed Bridwell. Mrs. Hartley identified Blanck as the man who checked into her boardinghouse on the day Bridwell was killed.

Blanck's attorney attempted to prove that he was insane. This defense was against Blanck's wishes as he considered living in a sanitarium even worse than a prison sentence. Bogue did not call any witnesses, but simply delivered a long speech, pleading for a second-degree murder charge.

But the jury didn't buy it. That Blanck murdered Bridwell seemed obvious. And his behavior during the trial, his smirks and laughter, did not endear him to the jury. It took them only thirty-five minutes to decide that Blanck was guilty of first-degree murder. On October 20, he was sentenced to hang on December 7.

As his hanging date drew near, the state supreme court decided to hear his appeal. Unfortunately for Blanck, the state supreme court upheld the decision of the lower court. Still, it was enough to delay the execution. Besides, Blanck wasn't done creating a sensation in Seattle.

On March 17, 1895, he escaped from the Seattle jail. He carved a revolver from a piece of broom handle and a piece of a shelf. He covered the wood with tin foil from a cigarette package to make it shiny. He made a knife out of a shoe shank to whittle the wood. He used some broken glass to polish the gun. When jailer Jerry Yerbury came to lock the prisoners up for the night, Blanck forced him to open the door to the cell. In the gloomy light, the jailer couldn't tell that the mock gun wasn't real. Blanck tied him up and locked him in the cell. He took the jailer's gun and his hat. He also took his keys and all the money he had. He took a coat from another inmate. Then Blanck and ten other inmates escaped.

As soon as they were out of sight, inmates James Murphy and William A. Wilcox ran to police headquarters and told them about the breakout. Cudihee and Phillips rushed to the scene immediately. They ran into another inmate, W. A. Wilcox, on their way. He had the fake gun and he gave it to Cudihee. They continued on to the jail where they released Yerbury. Sheriff Aaron T. Van de Vanter telegraphed the news all over the state and sent police to comb the area.

Most of the inmates had scattered in all directions, but Blanck and Servius Rutan stayed together. The two men followed Seventh Street to Yesler, then continued on toward the Grant Street Bridge. Some tramps held them up and stole the money that Blanck had stolen from the jailer. While walking along, they were spotted by deputies Michael Kelly and Thomas Burkman. The deputies captured Rutan, but Blanck got away.

One by one, the escaped jailbirds were captured. All of them confirmed that Blanck had planned the escape by himself. They had just taken advantage of it. Meanwhile Blanck reached the Black River Junction. He stopped at a schoolhouse to ask for food. Ella Nitcher told him she had no food, but to ask next door. The neighbor gave Blanck some food. Blanck continued on his way.

He continued south toward Renton. There he asked some children for some food, which they gave him. Then he headed farther south toward Kent. Later that evening, someone spotted him at a farmhouse near Auburn, so he circled back north toward Orillia. On March 21, he stopped at the farmhouse of James S. Nelson and demanded something to eat. After he left, Nelson wired the authorities that he had just seen Blanck.

While walking along a railroad track near Kent, deputies Robert Crow and John Shepich approached him. Shepich told him to put up his hands. Blanck paid no attention to him. Shepich repeated his demand. Blanck stopped walking and asked him what was going on. Shepich did not answer his question but told him again to put up his hands. Blanck drew his gun and fired at Shepich's head. His shot missed and allowed Shepich to fire his own gun. Crow also fired at him. Blanck returned his fire.

Several more shots were exchanged. Blanck fired his last bullet, then turned and ran down the embankment and fled along the east side of the tracks. Shepich yelled at him to give up. Amazingly, Blanck stopped running and held up his hands. Even though Blanck had his hands up, Shepich, Crow, and Charley Newell, who had just come on the scene, all fired at Blanck. Several shots hit him and a few minutes later, Blanck drew his last breath.

After his death, the residents of Seattle found out just how bad Blanck really was. It seems the murders of Jeffery and Bridwell were just part of a long list of crimes that he had committed during his lifetime. In 1890, he shot a police officer at Fairhaven near the Canadian border after stealing a suit of clothes. He escaped from jail at Fairhaven and headed east. He robbed a stagecoach in British Columbia and killed the driver. He had participated in several hold-ups in California. He robbed stages and banks all across Montana in 1894. He came north again and committed a burglary in Kalama, Washington, near the Columbia River, where he was captured and later escaped.

Another mystery may have been cleared up by Blanck's capture and death. In 1889, at South Bend, Washington, Mr.

and Mrs. Jens Fredericksen had been killed by some men known as George Rose, John Rose, John Edwards, and a Mr. Gibbons. While being held for trial, Mr. Gibbons and George Rose escaped from jail and were never caught. Though he denied it, Seattle police suspected that Blanck was none other than George Rose. The physical characteristics were very close to the same and the timing was right. However, too much time had passed for him to be positively identified.

By his capture and trial in Seattle, Blanck's outlaw days were done. His body was shipped back to Seattle on a train. There was a huge mob scene at the depot to get a look at the man who had terrorized the city. King County Coroners Oliver P. Askam and William C. Gibson conducted an autopsy. They found three shots that could have been fatal. The spectators followed his coffin all the way to the morgue. Thousands of people viewed the body at the mortuary. He was later buried without fanfare on March 25, 1895.

Frank Leroy

The small towns of Okanogan County were sparsely settled in the early 1900s, until mineral strikes brought flocks of miners to the area. As usual, the gold camps also attracted unsavory characters. One of them was Frank Leroy.

Leroy had committed a number of crimes in Washington by the time he arrived in the Okanogan country. He started his life of crime in the Seattle area and worked his way east. By the time anybody had connected the crimes to this lone operator, he had made his way to Brewster, in north-central Washington.

Early on the morning of November 4, 1909, Leroy broke into the A. C. Gillespie & Son store, blew up the safe there, and stole some knives. The next night, he broke into the home of William Plemmons and stole a gun, a lady's gold watch, and some other items. Plemmons followed some tracks around his house but found no one. A man driving the local stage saw a suspicious man following the road from Okanogan (city) to Brewster, but the stranger ducked out of sight when the stage got close. The footprints Plemmons discovered led in the direction of the stage road, so everyone guessed that the person the stage driver saw was the same person who had robbed Plemmons.

For a few days the thief eluded the law. Unfortunately for him, he didn't go any farther than Conconully, a town about thirty miles from Brewster. Both towns were located in Okanogan County, and the county sheriff was on the lookout for the robber. Leroy checked into a hotel on November 6 and stayed for dinner. For some reason his black hair and auburn mustache attracted the attention of the hotel managers. As they watched him, they noticed that he was wearing a gun. They sent someone to alert the sheriff, Fred Thorp.

The following day Leroy hung around the local saloons, secretly looking for a business to rob. One possibility was the Commercial Bank. Its location right next to his hotel would make his getaway easy. But before he could make his next move, he was accosted by the sheriff. Leroy made up a story that he was there to work on the government dam that was being built at the time. Sheriff Thorp accepted his story, but he and his deputy, Charles McLean, decided to keep an eye on Leroy.

The matter continued to bother Thorp, so he decided to talk to Leroy again. The next day, he found him in the Lute Morris Saloon. Though it was early in the day, an animated card game was already in progress. Thorp calmly told Leroy that he would have to accompany him to the sheriff's office so he could ask him some more questions. At first Leroy seemed to comply, but then he went for his gun.

Thorp and Leroy fired at each other at the same time. Somehow they both missed their targets, and their bullets harmed no one else in the barroom. Leroy ran around the saloon, making sure someone was between him and the sheriff's bullets at all times. As he headed for the back door, he felt a bullet graze his hand. The blow shocked him for a minute, and he dropped his gun. Before Thorp could take advantage of the moment, Leroy drew another gun from his pocket and headed out the door. As Leroy fled, Thorp shot him solidly in the upper back. This whole incident seemed to point to his guilt.

Leroy was now injured twice and was bleeding. He wasn't going to get far before the loss of blood began to affect him. He headed down Salmon Creek but managed to stumble only a few yards before he collapsed in some brush. He decided that small shelter would have to be a good enough hiding spot since that was as far as he could go.

Thorp and some other men went after him. Evidently Leroy could see Thorp before Thorp could see him. Leroy was just about to shoot when Thorp discovered his hiding spot and kicked the gun out of his hand. Leroy fell to the side and passed out from pain.

Some men laid Leroy's body on a piece of wood that used to be a barn door and carried him to the hotel. Undertaker Leonard Bragg, some deputies, and two doctors made sure Leroy didn't try to run again. The doctors noted that one of the bullets had gone clear through his shoulder and passed out his chest. As it passed through his body, the bullet punctured his lung. While the doctors looked at him, deputies searched Leroy's hotel room. They found two more guns, a set of burglary tools, some nitroglycerin, a lantern, fuse, wax, cotton batting, and a safecracker. They also found some of the items that had been stolen from the Gillespie store and Plemmons's home.

Dr. A. M. Polk declared that Leroy would live to stand trial. The deputies hauled him to the county jail just a short way down the road. With his injuries, they didn't figure he was going anywhere, so instead of putting him in a cell, they laid him on a cot in the corridor where there was more heat. The county did not have a regular jailer, so old Ed Braman, serving a few weeks' time for drunkenness, was assigned to look after Leroy. Braman was a "trusty," assigned to do odd jobs around the jailhouse. One of his tasks was to go to the Myers Hotel, where he picked up food for the jail inmates. Braman was locked up with Leroy at night.

Not long after his capture, Leroy stole Braman's pocketknife, broke the lock on the door to the corridor, and escaped the jail. As soon as he had the door open, he looked around for his clothes but couldn't find them. He stole Braman's shoes, an old brown coat, and a blanket, then he fled on foot. For some reason Braman woke up about four in the morning, discovered that Leroy was gone, and ran to the sheriff's house to alert him. The sheriff left his home immediately and headed for the jail.

Snow had fallen overnight, so Thorp hoped he might find footprints that would lead him to the outlaw. Unfortunately, all the footprints belonged to other citizens of the town. Thorp and McLean looked all over town trying to find Leroy. Thorp posted a $100 reward for his capture. Some thought that Leroy must have had help because he was still so weak from his injuries. Some even suspected that Braman might have been in on it. In any event, most people felt he would not be at large for long because of his wounds, the cold, and his lack of familiarity with the countryside.

In the meantime, Leroy followed the main road most of the day, keeping a couple hundred yards out of sight. That night he slept in a barn at Okanogan at least fifteen miles away from Conconully. With his injuries, it seemed impossible for Leroy to have traveled that far on foot. This fact later added to the suspicion that someone had helped him escape. He followed the main road, occasionally making a fire for warmth. Casper Miller owned a cabin in that area, and Leroy helped himself to its contents. He took some underclothes, pants, canned goods, crackers, a can opener, and a butcher knife. These tools and provisions helped him continue his flight even farther south. For three days and nights, he managed to stay out of sight of the law.

Thorp finally found Leroy hiding in some sagebrush near the Malott schoolhouse, another seven or eight miles south of Okanogan. Thorp told him to surrender. Leroy was unarmed and did as he was told.

Thorp and McLean escorted the criminal to Okanogan, where they stayed for the night. In the morning they took Leroy to Conconully and locked him in a holding cell in the jail. Thorp had been humane before, but that kindness had only caused him a lot of trouble. For the rest of his jail stay, Leroy spent his time in an uncomfortable, cold cell.

While waiting for Leroy's trial date, Thorp and prosecutor P. D. Smith investigated their unsavory tenant. It seemed he was a habitual criminal. Thorp compared the pictures of men named Charles Ray, Andrew Morgan, and Frank Leroy and saw that they were the same man. Only the most outrageous coincidence could account for all three men having a partially deformed right hand and a tattoo of a nude woman chained to a tree on the inside of their right forearm. Under the name Andrew Morgan, Leroy had been sent to prison in September 1899 for a burglary in Coupeville on Whidbey Island. He was released on December 18, 1900. He eluded the law until May 1903, when he served time for a burglary in Skagit County. He was using the name Charles Ray at the time. His stay was longer this time, just over six years. He had been released from the Walla Walla prison less than a month before he had burglarized the store and home in Brewster.

Leroy was arraigned on December 6. A court-appointed attorney represented him. He pled not guilty, and the trial

(left to right) Robber Frank Leroy and Deputy Charles McLean.
(Okanogan County Historical Society)

was set for January 11, 1910. On January 4, Leroy's counsel resigned, and the court had to appoint a new lawyer. This attorney tried to get a continuance, stating that he had been unable to secure witnesses. But the court denied this motion, filed on January 6. The court ruled that Leroy had had ample time to secure his two witnesses, one in Clark County and the other at Spokane. The trial commenced on January 11, 1910, as originally scheduled.

Plemmons and the stage driver testified at the trial, putting Leroy in the vicinity of the burglary at the correct time. Another man testified to seeing a man of Leroy's description in Brewster the day before the store was robbed. A. C. Gillespie described the break-in of his store and produced the key that was taken from Leroy. This key unlocked the back door of the store, Gillespie said. He also identified the knives in Leroy's possession as coming from his store.

After an hour of deliberation, the jury found Leroy guilty of second-degree burglary. Since it was his third burglary conviction, Judge Taylor sentenced him to life in prison as a habitual criminal. Leroy appealed the decision to the state supreme court. Twisp attorney E. C. Jennings handled the appeal. His contention was that the court erred in the jury selection. Jurors had been selected in November for December. Because there were no cases to be heard in December, the same jurors were held over for the January trials. These jurors were the ones who heard Leroy's case. Leroy and Jennings claimed this fact prejudiced the case. The state supreme court disagreed with that argument and upheld the decision of the lower court. Two weeks later, Leroy was on his way to Walla Walla for the last time.

Leroy stayed in prison for nearly nine years. Part of that time he was sick with "inflammatory rheumatism" and could not work. Acting governor Louis Hart granted him a conditional parole, and he was released from prison on November 15, 1919. After that Leroy left the state. No one knows exactly what happened to him after that, but the Thorp family believes he died of tuberculosis.

John Tornow

Though he was busy butchering a steer, John Tornow listened closely to the forest around him. Suddenly, the quiet was interrupted by some noises in the dense underbrush. A shot rang out, followed by more noise. Tornow thought someone was firing at him. He quickly stood up and looked around. He saw shadows moving in the brush and fired at them. After he fired once, the first shadow dropped. He fired again, and though he hit his mark, the second shadow still stood. He fired one more time, and the shadow fell to the ground. Feeling confident that he was no longer in danger, Tornow went to have a closer look. What he saw astonished him.

The two men he had just shot were his nineteen-year-old twin nephews, William and John Bauer. Though he was sorry about their deaths, his self-protective instinct kicked in. He knew the incident would make him a wanted man. He used a broken limb to dig shallow trenches in the soft, pine-needle-covered earth. He placed the bodies in the shallow graves and gently laid dirt and branches over the top to hide them. Then he disappeared, leaving behind the half-butchered steer and retreating deeper into the woods of Grays Harbor and Mason Counties.

How did John Tornow come to this desperate situation? Perhaps it all started during his childhood. About 1870, Fritz and Louisa Tornow moved to Washington state and bought a 320-acre homestead on the Satsop River about midway between the small towns of Matlock and Brady. They would eventually have six children: Edward, Frederick, Albert,

William, John (born September 4, 1880), and Minnie. In 1890 Tornow contracted a severe case of black measles. His condition was precarious, but he pulled through. The doctor warned his parents that the high fevers might have caused permanent brain damage. They saw no immediate evidence of it, however.

Because she almost lost him and she had already lost two other children in infancy, John Tornow's mother doted on him. This caused hard feelings among the other children, especially the youngest boy, Edward. He resented all the attention his older brother received. Their father went out of his way to teach the boy how to hunt and fish. He taught him survival skills and showed him how to track and how to hide his own tracks. Fritz Tornow hoped to help his son develop self-confidence and to become more comfortable around people. Unfortunately, the scheme did not work. John Tornow showed less and less inclination to spend time around people, preferring to spend time in the woods. His best friend was his dog, Cougar.

He attended school for a short while and for the most part was a good student. But he was shy and did not associate with the other children very much. The other schoolchildren thought him odd because he spent so much time in the woods. He developed a lisp. Some kids made fun of him and called him names, which made him withdraw even more.

By the time he was twelve, he could hunt all his own food. He claimed he could understand bird calls. He could also imitate many bird and animal calls. He could make clothes out of animal hides and burlap and make shoes from bark. Some accounts claim that he became so unmanageable that his parents sent him to a sanitarium. Modern researchers have been unable to uncover any evidence of this, however.

As he grew older, he couldn't stand to be in a crowd. He did not like to feel closed in. He would not go inside a store or other building unless it had a very high ceiling. Even then, he would do his business as quickly as he could. He was very bashful, but cheerful. He was often afraid that people were picking on him.

Tornow's older sister Minnie married a man named Henry Bauer. Their two girls, Lizzie and Mary, were only a few years younger than John Tornow. Twins John and William were born when Tornow was twelve. Though they lived a few miles away from the Tornow homestead, Minnie continued to spend time at her parents' home, helping her mother with household chores and taking care of her younger brothers. Her husband did not like her spending so much time at the homestead because he was very jealous of Fritz Tornow. Fritz had a nicer home and more money than his son-in-law. The senior Tornow had been able to pay off all his debts by selling some of the timber on his property. He also had surplus crops that he could sell for a little extra spending money. After Fritz Tornow died in 1909, the Bauers' daughter Mary moved in with the Tornows to help her mother and grandmother. Henry Bauer became even more resentful.

While Minnie was busy trying to hold her marriage together and helping her mother with the chores, John Tornow moved to the woods to stay. He had reached his full height of over six feet and weighed over two hundred pounds. Occasionally he would visit Minnie; he doted on his two nephews, passing on to them what he knew of the woods.

In August 1911, John visited the old homestead near Satsop. While there, he found out that his brother Ed had shot his old hunting dog, claiming that it was too old to hunt anymore.

The Fritz Tornow family, photographed against a log cabin wall, approximately 1893. Standing left to right: Albert, John, Minnie, Frederick, and William Tornow. Sitting left to right: Louisa, Edward, and Fritz Tornow. *(Courtesy Ron Fowler, Steilacoom, Washington)*

Tornow was enraged. In revenge, he shot Ed's dog, Rex. He warned Ed never to come after him or to send anyone after him, or he would be sorry. On August 11, Ed went to Sheriff Mark Payette and swore out a warrant for his brother's arrest. He wanted his brother committed. The sheriff could find no basis for the arrest. But the incident didn't help John Tornow's reputation any.

He retreated again to the woods, where he built a series of lean-tos and shacks and used them for shelters while he was out trapping. He set his traps between the Wynoochee and Satsop Rivers. He stayed in the woods for months at a time, only occasionally coming to town to visit the family homestead or his sister's house. He occasionally brought game and traded it for flour or salt.

Then came that fateful day in 1911. On September 3, the Bauer twins were out hunting for bear. A bear had recently killed one of their cows. Stories differ on whether Tornow shot the twins by accident or on purpose. Some accounts state that the incident took place in an area that had already been logged, so it should have been clear to Tornow exactly who he was shooting at. Others say that the undergrowth was too dense for Tornow to have seen clearly who was there, but not dense enough that he couldn't hit what he was aiming at. Whatever the case, the twins died by his hand.

When the boys did not return that night, Minnie was worried. Henry Bauer went out to look for them. The next day he rode into Matlock and asked Sheriff Payette to search for the missing twins. Deputies Colin McKenzie and Carl Swartz led a posse to the homestead. With them were Ed Maas and his bloodhounds to aid in the search. Unfortunately, rainfall the previous night had washed away most of the trail, so the dogs proved ineffectual.

The next day the deputies returned to the cabin to continue the search for the Bauer twins. The situation began to look promising when the dogs picked up the scent of a bear. Since the Bauers had gone out to hunt bear, the officers thought it a good idea to follow the trail. Perhaps the Bauer boys would be at the other end of it, too busy butchering a bear to notice the time. The bear had been wounded so it shouldn't be too far away.

Deputy McKenzie paused for a rest when he noticed a pile of tree limbs. It looked unnatural to him. Loggers didn't leave limbs in piles; they scattered them all around. He pushed the limbs aside and started digging. Almost immediately he knew he'd found the missing twins. William had been shot once in the heart. John had been hit twice, once in the head and once in the stomach. Two empty cartridges were found nearby. So was the steer that Tornow had been butchering. A short distance away was a small shelter that Tornow had probably used. McKenzie left the bodies where he found them and returned to town to get the sheriff and the coroner, R. F. Hunter.

At first the attention did not focus on John Tornow, though he was a suspect. Some thought Tornow's brother Ed might try to get him into trouble because of his intense jealousy of John. The fact that Ed had tried to have his brother committed added to the suspicion. Ed had also been in some trouble with Henry Bauer when Bauer's daughter Mary had become pregnant out of wedlock. Ed took her to Aberdeen to have the baby, hoping to keep the secret from her father. Unfortunately, she died after an attempted abortion. Henry blamed Ed for the death of his daughter, and he may have been justified. If Ed resented being blamed, he could have killed the twins to get back at Henry.

Another likely suspect was Henry himself. He may have suspected the twins were not his biological sons. One of the times that Minnie had visited her father's house, a man had been visiting there, and she had struck up a conversation with him. While waiting for her father to return, the two had gone into the forest to pick berries. As a result, there was always speculation about whether she had been intimate with the man. If so, perhaps Henry could no longer tolerate the sight of her infidelity.

There was also the matter of the Tornow property. Upon his father's death, John Tornow had inherited $1,700 as well as the land. Perhaps Bauer killed the boys deliberately to throw suspicion on Tornow. Perhaps Tornow could be taken out of the picture so that Minnie somehow would end up with the property.

Not long after the death of the Bauer twins, Henry Bauer disappeared and was never seen again. That left only John Tornow to be blamed for their deaths. The sheriff assembled a posse to hunt for him. Payette chose McKenzie, Swartz, and Deputies Philbrick, Hildebrand, Elliott, and Bonnell to help him.

A week passed before anyone found any sign of Tornow. Two lumbermen, Mike Scully and Earl McIntosh, were out camping when Tornow approached them. They told him that he was the chief suspect in the Bauer twins' murder. He denied it flatly, saying that he had too much love and respect for them. He told them to tell everyone what he said and that they should leave him alone.

Unfortunately, the law had by then decided that Tornow was to blame. They no longer tried to investigate anyone else. Some townspeople doubted that Tornow had killed the boys, and others felt that if he had killed them, it was surely an accident.

McKenzie continued to search along the Wynoochee for signs of Tornow's whereabouts. Deputy Swartz searched the Deckerville area. Occasionally they found caches of food or a smoldering campfire. But by the end of the year, no one had seen Tornow or a place where he could be living. Other stories circulated regarding Tornow's whereabouts. One lead said that he had been seen on Mount Olympus. As unlikely as that seemed, some deputies climbed seven thousand feet before heavy snow turned them back. Another search party combed the west side of the Humptulips River. Yet another team searched around Quinault Lake. Four trappers on the Wishkah River claimed Tornow had burned down their shack. A hunter said a man woke him up at midnight demanding salt and pepper. Some men who worked for the Simpson Logging Company said they had seen him several times. Others claimed they saw him haunting saloons at Montesano.

But try as he might, the sheriff could not find Tornow. The sheriff finally called off the search until the weather improved. That winter was very severe, and some thought that the exposure would kill Tornow. But Tornow was used to surviving in the woods. He spent part of that winter in a schoolhouse, beneath the flooring of the schoolroom. He removed two loose boards from the floor so he could easily come and go. He also took shelter in a huge, dead cedar that fishermen called "the big tree on the Satsop." At least ten feet in diameter, it was hollow near the ground.

But Tornow knew the law would be out after him again in the spring, so he killed a large elk and dressed it out to last him for several weeks. He built a camouflaged lean-to by two downed tree trunks up next to a hillside. The root balls blocked the view of his shelter.

In March 1912, trappers Louis Blair and Frank Getty came across the remains of the elk Tornow had butchered near the Mason County line. The way it was carefully butchered to preserve the most meat led them to believe that the kill belonged to Tornow. They reported what they found to Sheriff Payette.

Payette sent McKenzie and a game warden named A. V. Elmer to look for Tornow, telling them not to try to catch

Tornow, but to just see if they could find him. All through the day, McKenzie and Elmer felt as if they were being watched. If Tornow was out there, they wished he would show himself. But after a day of searching they found nothing. They spent the night in an old trapper's cabin. The next day they followed an elk trail. At the end of the trail, they found a half-butchered elk carcass. Human footprints led away from it toward a ridge.

Elmer got excited, thinking they were on the verge of catching up with Tornow. He was ready to go back and lead the posse to that location. McKenzie insisted on looking for further proof. He would soon wish he hadn't. A few minutes later they crawled under a fallen log too big to crawl over. Just on the other side was Tornow's hideout. As soon as Tornow had a good shot, he fired. He killed Elmer with a shot through the heart. McKenzie tried to dodge behind cover, but it was too late. Tornow shot him twice, killing him.

If Tornow wasn't guilty of murder before, he was definitely guilty now. He had enough of his wits about him to know he had to get rid of the evidence fast. He quickly stripped the bodies of their clothes and shoes to replace his own ragged clothing. He took their guns and ammunition and the biscuits they were carrying in their knapsack. He dragged them to a spot about fifteen feet from where they fell. Then he buried the bodies in a shallow grave on the hillside. Their bodies were placed in the shape of a letter T.

Payette became concerned when he didn't hear anything from McKenzie and Elmer. He sent a posse led by Deputy A. L. Fitzgerald, Blair, and Deputy Charles Lathrop to look for the men. They found the elk carcass and the tracks that led away from it. Fitzgerald came upon Tornow's abandoned camp near the headwaters of the Wynoochee. They searched the camp and found some empty shell casings that were the same kind as those found by the Bauer boys' bodies. They also found some smoked meat and flour and some remnants of the Bauers' clothing. A few minutes later, they stumbled across the buried bodies of McKenzie and Elmer. Both were shot through the heart.

The posse went back to town to fetch the sheriff and Coroner Hunter. The officials and some others arrived the next day and transported the two bodies back to town. The county commissioners posted a $4,000 reward for the capture of Tornow. Previously they had refused to post a reward on the grounds that there was no proof he had killed the Bauer twins. But there seemed to be no doubt that he killed the deputy and the game warden. The governor posted another $1,000 reward for the capture of Tornow.

Immediate searches proved fruitless, but then Tornow was seen on the county road about two hundred yards from his old home. He stood there just long enough for some young men in a car to get a good look at him. As soon as Tornow saw the car, he disappeared into the brush.

Francis Gleason and four other young men said that Tornow looked haggard. His dark hair was tangled, and he wore a bushy beard. He was wearing a well-worn canvas hunting coat, possibly the one Elmer was wearing when he went after Tornow. He did not appear to be carrying a gun. When Gleason told his father about what he saw, the elder Gleason was sure it was Tornow. He used to hunt and fish with Tornow, so he knew him well.

But the sighting led to nothing but more reported sightings. People let their imaginations get the best of them as they reported Tornow sightings all over the Olympic Peninsula. His story was written up in newspapers across the country, where he was given such monikers as "wild man" and "cougar man." Sightings were reported as far away as Port Angeles. One day he was reportedly seen at Pacific Beach, the next at Olympia, the next at Elma. Someone even claimed they saw him at Clallam Bay, but someone else claimed he was in jail in Chehalis the same day. Supposedly someone broke into a building at Simpson Logging Camp No. 5 and stole boots. Soon every incident of a missing person was blamed on Tornow, without any evidence whatsoever. The newspapers even tried to pin the disappearance of two prospectors on Tornow. They had disappeared sometime in 1910, before the death of the Bauer twins.

In actuality, Tornow had retreated deeper into the forest. He only came down from the hills occasionally to beg for food from homesteaders. Most gave it willingly because they were sympathetic.

In January 1913, Schelle Mathews was elected sheriff on the promise that he would bring in Tornow. On his first day in office Sheriff Mathews led Bob Crinklaw, Louis Retsloff, George Stormes, Con Elliot, and Giles Quimby on a manhunt, hoping that footprints in the snow would lead him to Tornow. But they found nothing. It wasn't until April, when Mathews was riding the train home from Tacoma, that he got his first real break. A real estate developer from Hoquiam, named J. B. Lucas, gave him some very interesting information: He described a small lake with a small cabin. A log laid across the water to an island in the lake. Lucas stumbled across this area one day and thought to himself that it might be a hideout for a wild man.

Immediately upon his return to Matlock, Mathews sent Deputy Giles Quimby, his brother-in-law, to capture Tornow. Quimby had served in the Spanish-American War of 1898 and was known to be tough and clever. Mathews also hired Stormes, Elliot, Charles Lathrop, and Blair. Quimby, Lathrop, and Blair went ahead with Lathrop's Airedale to help track down Tornow. Eventually the three men reached a cabin deep in the woods, and inside they found the old prospector who had said he had seen Tornow asleep. They spent the night at the cabin, hoping to catch up to Tornow the next day, April 16, 1913.

Quimby wanted to wait for the others, but Blair and Lathrop thought Tornow would get away. Against his better judgment, Quimby followed them into the woods. They hiked around a small lake, through a bog, and over a marsh full of horsetail plants. They circled the lake, keeping an eye on a lean-to on an island in the lake. They spotted some smoke coming out of the lean-to.

They thought Tornow might still be close by, and he was. What they didn't know was that Tornow had a built-in warning system on his little island. He had placed a log across the water so that he could walk across it from the island back to the mainland. Some frogs near the log normally croaked constantly. But whenever anyone came near, they stopped. Tornow had heard the sudden silence and had looked to see who had come near. As soon as he was behind cover, he began firing. He shot Blair first and killed him with the first round. Lathrop dove for cover and then started firing in Tornow's direction. They exchanged a few shots before Lathrop exposed himself just a little too much. He too soon fell victim to Tornow's gun. Both men had been shot in the forehead.

Quimby kept firing until he was sure he had shot Tornow. He quickly reloaded, then listened. The only sound was the chirping of birds. Perhaps he had hit Tornow, but he wasn't sticking around to find out. He crawled a hundred yards or so, staying out of sight. When he thought he was out of range, he ran for Simpson Logging Camp No. 5, about four miles away. Mathews waited there with the gathering posse.

The next day Mathews led about two dozen men back to the lake. Quimby showed them the way. He figured that, even if Tornow had survived and escaped, eventually he would come back to this base camp, at which point they could catch him. After searching the small island, they found the bodies of Blair and Lathrop. Then they found the body of the outlaw. Tornow was, in fact, dead. The "Wild Man of the Wynoochee" was no more. Quimby's bullet had hit him just above the breastbone and had lodged in his right shoulder. Later Quimby would be awarded a third of the reward money, but it is unknown whether he actually collected it.

Tornow wore several layers of ragged clothes and good boots he stole from one of his victims. He wore six shirts and five pairs of pants. The posse members also searched his campsite, where they found a few silver coins, some tools, some gunnysacks, and plenty of matches. They also found McKenzie's watch. They did not find any food.

The body was taken back to Montesano and put on public display. Tornow was later buried at Satsop next to his parents and his nephews. He died with almost $1,700 in the Montesano state bank. He owned two lots in Aberdeen and a fifth of the old homestead.

In 1987, seventy-five years later, Tornow garnered sympathy from the townspeople. A marker was made for Tornow's grave. The grave is in the family cemetery, nine and a half miles north of Highway 12, off the Brady–Matlock Road. The "Ballad of John Tornow" was sung at a special ceremony. The inscription on the gray granite monument reads: From Loner to Outcast to Fugitive, John Tornow, Sept 4, 1880–April 16, 1913.

The Great Nude Bathing Case

The early part of the twentieth century was a time of great political upheaval. The United States was climbing out of the financial collapse of 1893, and in a prelude to the 1960s, young and old alike were questioning how government was running the country. Little pockets of "resistance" started springing up all over the country. One such resistance community was the small town of Home, Washington, which was located on Van Geldern Cove, on the Kitsap Peninsula.

Only a few settlers lived in this remote area when three men rowed across Puget Sound from Tacoma. They previously had been living in a nearby socialist community called Glennis, formed in 1896. But internal strife in the town caused George Allen, O. A. Verity, and F. F. Odell to seek out their own perfect community.

The place they found was completely undeveloped. There were no roads, but there was a nice beach with Douglas fir surrounding it. The three men bought twenty-six acres for $7 an acre. They made a down payment of $20 on the land, and dug clams and sold timber in Tacoma to pay the rest. In 1897 the three men returned to Van Geldern Cove with their wives and children. They cut down some trees and built cabins along this calm body of water.

The three men formed a compact, which they called the Mutual Home Colony Association. They considered their settlement an anarchist colony. The purpose of the association was "to obtain land and to promote better social and moral conditions." Each member paid the association to use two acres of land. The land remained the property of the association, but the members could live there indefinitely by paying taxes imposed by the "enemy," which was the state and the country. Certificates of membership were held for life and could be willed. The only other rule for the colonists was to remember tolerance.

After six months, six more families joined the Verity, Allen, and Odell families on the island. The men built Liberty Hall, which they used as a meeting place and school. George Allen was the first teacher.

Verity started a newspaper and called it *New Era*. He printed it on a portable press with some type that he found at a secondhand store in Tacoma. His goal was not to tell Home about the world around it, but to tell the world about Home, Washington. There weren't many subscribers, but the publishers sent many free copies to those who might be interested. The paper's primary point was free love, and this attitude and publicity attracted all kinds of "crackpots" to the colony. The original colonists were too busy establishing the town to pay much attention to the new arrivals.

Charles Govan and James F. Morton Jr. came to town and started a new newspaper called *Discontent, Mother of Progress*. Both men had newspaper experience, but the new paper seemed to contain a lot of articles about sex. Henry Addis and Abner J. Pope had recently been in trouble for publishing the Portland paper *Firebrand*, which the courts had considered too obscene, so the two men moved to Home, where Addis began writing for *Discontent*.

Then an incident that occurred in Buffalo, New York, produced a long-lasting impact on Home. President William

McKinley was assassinated in Buffalo on September 6, 1901. The assassin, Leon Czolgosz, was said to be an anarchist, so the incident gave peaceful anarchists a bad name. Suddenly Home came under public scrutiny. A meeting was held in Tacoma to speak out against Home. Some citizens formed the "Loyalty League" and made plans to do away with Home. They accused the colonists of keeping community wives and committing various crimes from arson to murder. They took weapons in hand, ready to terrorize the colony. They wanted to burn the place down, even if people were injured or killed in the fire.

Ed Lorenz, a steamboat captain, calmed down the mob. He piloted the regular ferry to Home and had seen that the people were basically peaceful and industrious. He knew that none of them had ever spent time in a jail. Lorenz also warned the people of Home about the vigilante committee. Reverend J. F. Doescher also vouched for the community after observing the people. He said they were sober, industrious, and friendly, and he felt Home residents were being better citizens than those who were condemning them. Fortunately, the ire of the mob died down, and nothing happened.

But that was not the end of Home's troubles. By then, federal authorities had noticed *Discontent* and were outraged because the paper printed articles against marriage and for premarital sex. A U.S. marshal went to Home to arrest the paper's editors and contributors. The colonists met him at the wharf, fed him supper, and held a big dance in his honor. But their hospitality didn't deter him. The next morning he arrested Govan and his two assistants and took them to Tacoma.

The three men were tried on March 11, 1902. Federal Judge Cornelius Hanford ordered the jury to return a verdict of not guilty, but in April, the postmaster general closed the Home post office and banned mailing of the paper. This event occurred partly because Mattie Penhallow, postmistress at the time, told the postmaster general that she was an anarchist.

All this excitement surrounding Home attracted a lot of attention in the national press. Even more people came to live at the colony. One of them was Henry Dadisman, a wealthy farmer from Virginia. He bought land, then leased it back to other settlers. A Minnesota widow came and built a nice farmhouse. A few other families arrived from Indiana, and a group of Russian Jews came to escape persecution. This influx of people required a larger Liberty Hall, and a new co-op store was opened. The town was platted that year.

The old newspaper had been banned, but that didn't stop the publishers from printing. They simply changed the name of the paper and published the same content as before. The new paper was called *Demonstrator* and was distributed to a national audience. Lois Waisbrooker also published an outrageous rag named *Clothed With The Sun*. As soon as the post office got a look at a copy, she was arrested and fined. She simply returned to Home and published a different paper called *Foundation Principles*, with the same material.

All the publicity attracted yet more eccentrics to Home. One man named Professor Thompson declared that the world would never reach perfection until all people wore women's clothing, since it was aesthetic and comfortable. Someone opened a school that taught Esperanto. Someone else taught a class in Hatha yoga. A woman named Laura Wood lived in an Indian wigwam. College professors studied the colony and wrote learned papers. Moses Harmon, editor of a paper called

Lucifer, came to Home after several stints in Illinois and Kansas prisons. Those sentences were served for advocating contraception in his paper.

Other oddball residents included friends Joe Kapella and Franz Erkelems, who came to Home looking for an ideal place to build a house. A spring nearby provided ample water, but the spring made the ground too soggy to support the weight of a building. So they cut down a large tree and built a house on top of the stump. They pitched a tent over the spring to serve as a kitchen and ice box. They laid their dirty dishes in the spring to be washed off by the flowing water and hungry minnows.

One of the more eccentric women of Home claimed that Count Tolstoi had given her a chalet. She was a vegetarian and wore odd clothes and jewelry, including a necklace of dyed ostrich plumes that looked like fur. She wore many rings that had crests of five different kings. One day she left town, leaving all her bills unpaid.

Liberty Hall engaged a large number of speakers. Bill Haywood, leader of the Wobblies (Industrial Workers of the World), came for a visit and delivered a few lectures. Elizabeth Gurley Flynn and Emma Goldman, well-known radicals, also spoke there. Sometimes the speakers started fads, and often the fads affected the butcher, John Buchi. When the speakers advocated a vegetarian diet, he had to sell his meat in Tacoma because no one in Home would buy it. But then someone else would expound on the virtues of raw beef, and he wouldn't have enough meat to serve the community. He would restock, then someone would speak on the value of fasting, and he would have too much stock on hand. This constant seesawing of sentiment was very hard on him. Eventually he became very ill and spent the rest of his life in the state mental hospital.

Once again the town outgrew Liberty Hall, so the villagers built Harmony Hall for dances and to use as a community hall. The town had no saloon, jail, or church, but it did have its own baseball team that played other small towns around Puget Sound such as Delano, Elgin, and Gig Harbor. Home also had a debating society and a band and offered classes in pencil drawing, watercolor, German, flower culture, and spiritualism.

The economy of Home was strong, too. Their most profitable commodity was timber, which they sold to steamships. They grew apples, plums, prunes, cherries, pears, crabapples, quince, and grapes. They sold wild blackberries and huckleberries, and shellfish. They also raised poultry. Other businesses included the Home Mercantile, a Morell Company outlet, the White Electric Soap Company, and the Dillon-Bragget Logging Company. The town became a port of call for a dozen boats.

But then stories started to circulate that sex orgies and nude bathing were going on at the colony. These rumors were in part deduced from *Demonstrator* articles. Residents of Tacoma took the daily ferry to Home to check out just how "disgusting" the nude bathing was. Then came the final showdown—a debacle that became known as the Great Nude Bathing Case of 1910.

Over time, the colony had split into two factions over a disagreement over land ownership. The disagreement was settled by awarding each member of the colony a deed to their two acres. The association was then dissolved, though Liberty Hall and the co-op store remained open. The co-op attracted some farmers from Lakebay because the prices were generally lower, but some of these farmers did not like that some members of the colony, men and women both, were bathing naked together. They reported it to the constable. Home did not like the complaints.

The charge was true. Certain members were bathing together. These were the Russian members of the commune, known as Dukhobors, who bathed together in their home country as a tradition. Their custom was to remove their clothes at home before heading to the beach, so at any time one might encounter a bare "Dukh" heading for the beach. The villagers took it all in stride. Some even joined them, but others didn't like it. The practice died down in the winter, when it was too cold for nude bathing, but the following spring it became an issue once again. Finally, Justice of the Peace Tom Lark of Lakebay arrested two men and two women for indecent exposure.

Then in October of 1910, the *Los Angeles Times* building was blown up, and the suspects were anarchists. Home was suspected of harboring the criminals. This was because one of the suspects had once lived at Home. J. M. Tillman, a detective from the Burns Detective Agency, came to Home to investigate the matter. After he filed his report, he left the agency and stayed on at Home as the local sheriff. He was the second detective to leave the Burns agency to live at Home. J. D. Sandusky also stayed at Home and later married a local girl.

By then, Jay Fox was publishing a new paper called *The Agitator*. On July 1, 1911, he published an editorial for the paper called "The Nudes and the Prudes," charging that all people who loved their freedom should reject those who had brought the charges against the nudists. He wrote that "no one went rubbernecking to see which suit a person wore, who sought the purifying waters of the bay. Surely it was nobody's business. All were sufficiently pure minded to see no vulgarity, no suggestion of anything vile or indecent in the thought of nature's masterpiece uncovered. But eventually a few prudes got into the community and proceeded in the brutal, unneighborly way of the outside world to suppress the people's freedom." He said the only thing Home did not tolerate was intolerance. He called for the freedom-loving colonists to boycott anyone who opposed the nudists.

Sheriff Tillman arrested Fox and took him to jail. The prosecuting attorney was upset when he saw that there had been a 200-percent increase in the number of arrests for nude bathing, and he attributed the increase to Fox's article. He chose to ignore that the hot summer season had brought more nude bathers out, not the article.

Fox's trial began on November 6, 1911, in the Pierce County Courthouse. A. O. Burmeister and G. C. Nolte prosecuted the case, claiming that the editorial "encouraged disrespect for the law" and that it encouraged nude bathing. Colonel J. J. Anderson defended Fox. Anderson stated that the editorial did not advocate disrespect for the law. He also wondered why the court was making such a big deal over this one newspaper when probably every newspaper in the state criticized the state and its laws. He said, "I'll tell you why you don't prosecute them. It's because they all control votes. They control money and influence. But Fox has none of these." The audience enjoyed his speech and broke out in applause.

The judge mulled over the case for several weeks. Eventually he left the decision up to the jury. The jury deliberated for twenty-five hours before declaring Fox guilty. They did, however, ask the judge to be lenient in his sentencing. The maximum penalty was a year in the county jail or a $1,000 fine, or both. On January 12, 1912, Fox was sentenced to two months in the county jail. In February, he appealed the case on the grounds that the law forbidding publication of inflammatory material was unconstitutional. He also claimed that the required sixty days had elapsed for filing charges against him. But the state supreme court upheld the conviction.

The U.S. Supreme Court refused to hear an appeal. So in February 1913, Fox finally served his two months at the Pierce County Jail. With two weeks to go in his sentence, Ernest Lister became governor. He pardoned Fox, being sympathetic to his cause.

Fox returned to Home and started publishing his paper again, but the bad publicity had affected Home's economy. People began moving away. Tillman resigned from office after several complaints were lodged against him by residents of Home because he had been on the side of the anti-nude-bathing faction. The paper stopped publishing, but Fox stayed on to write his memoirs. George Allen, one of the original founders, lived there until his death in 1944. A few other diehards stayed on, and the town of Home survived into the twenty-first century.

Harry Tracy

At seven o'clock on the morning of June 9, 1902, several dozen prisoners at Oregon State Penitentiary in Salem, Oregon, shuffled out of their cellblock on their way to the prison foundry. They worked eight hours every day making iron stoves. As far as the prison guards could tell, this day was just another ordinary day at work. The guards lined up the prisoners to be counted, but before they could finish the task, one prisoner, Harry Tracy, suddenly grabbed a hidden gun. Tracy started shooting, killing guard Frank B. Ferrell. Tracy's partner, Dave Merrill, grabbed another hidden weapon. When inmate Frank Ingram tried to stop him from using it, Merrill shot and wounded Ingram in the stomach. The rest of the inmates ducked down to get out of the way of the two felons. Rather than risk getting shot, two other guards, Frank Girard and John Stapleton, fled the foundry.

Tracy and Merrill ran out of the foundry, carrying ammunition and a rope ladder and firing at anyone who came near them. They ran for the prison wall and threw the rope ladder up over it. Several guards in the vicinity shot at them, but none of the shots met their mark. The escapees scrambled up and over the wall, still firing their weapons. Just before he went over the wall, Tracy shot and killed guard S. R. T. Jones, who patrolled the wall.

But Tracy and Merrill weren't free yet. Two guards jumped over the wall after them. Tracy anticipated this action and used them to shield himself and Merrill from anyone who tried to shoot at them. Tracy and Merrill dragged the guards as far as

Mill Creek, where B. F. Tiffany was either killed by Tracy or by a stray shot from another guard, and Duncan Ross was released unharmed. Tracy and Merrill had escaped.

The prison was a long way from Harry Tracy's hometown. He was born in about 1874 in Wood County, Wisconsin. His given name was Harry Severns. It is hard to imagine where he went wrong. He had had adequate role models in his childhood. His father was in the lumber business, and his grandfather served in the Civil War and held several government posts, including justice of the peace. His family and friends considered him good-hearted and intelligent. In fact, it was his brother Ervie who had been known as the troublemaker of the family.

As a teenager, Tracy worked as a cook at a logging camp owned by his friend John Goodwin. During one of his logging jobs, he worked for a man named Mike Tracy, and it is believed that Tracy adopted his new last name from that association.

Tracy's first brush with the law was probably during a wheat harvest in Fargo, North Dakota. He was twenty years old when he and some friends stole some money from another worker to go out for a night on the town. When the man discovered the theft, he called the local sheriff. A shootout ensued, but Tracy escaped. He headed west, on the run from the law.

Tracy arrived in Washington state in 1895. He took a job as a logger at Loon Lake, about forty miles north of Spokane. He worked there for about a year before he moved to Provo, Utah, where he was soon arrested for robbing a residence. He was convicted and sentenced to one year in jail. There, he met a man named David Lant, who was convicted of robbery. Tracy, Lant, and two others immediately started planning an escape.

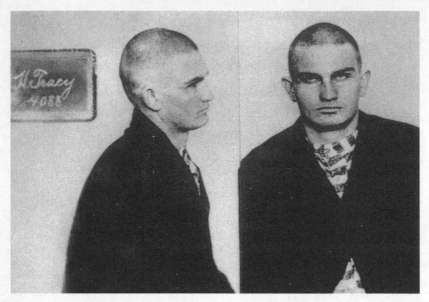

Harry Tracy at the time he entered the Oregon State Penitentiary in Salem in 1899.
(Courtesy Jim Dullenty, Hamilton, Montana)

On October 8, 1897, the four men were part of a ten-man chain gang digging ditches outside of Salt Lake City. Tracy led the escape by getting the drop on a guard named John Van Streeter with a carved gun covered with tinfoil.

The four men fled east, where they commandeered a horse and buggy from a man named H. A. Stearns. Tracy and Lant fled to Vernal, Utah, where they began a new career rustling horses. They soon moved north to Brown's Hole on the Wyoming–Utah–Colorado border, which was a haven for outlaws at the time.

When a posse came scouting for rustlers, Tracy and Lant fled with a man named Pat Johnson. The posse chased them to Douglas Mountain in western Colorado, where they took up a defensive position. As Tracy warned the posse not to come after them, Valentine Hoy, Pat Johnson's boss, cautiously approached their hideout. Hoy might not have been interested in Tracy and Lant, but he certainly wanted to talk to his employee, who was wanted for murder in another state. Tracy decided to show the posse he meant business, so he shot and killed Hoy. In the confusion, the outlaws escaped again. But not for long.

The next day, the posse caught up with them. Johnson received a one-way ticket to Wyoming to stand trial there for murder. Tracy and Lant were locked up in the Routt County, Colorado, jail, but they overpowered the sheriff and escaped. Only a day later, the sheriff captured them and transported them to the Pitkin County jail at Aspen, a more substantial building than that in Routt County. But they managed to break out of that, too. Using an old trick, Tracy whittled a gun out of soap and covered it with tinfoil. After that, Lant disappeared, ending his association with Harry Tracy.

Tracy was on his own again. He fled back to Washington State, where he began a new crime spree in Seattle. He robbed streetcar conductors and bartenders to survive. He robbed the guests of several hotels, especially those who he determined were wealthy. He kept just ahead of the law as he gradually worked his way south. Eventually he arrived in Portland, Oregon. While there, he met Dave Merrill, a small-time crook. The two men teamed up, committing several robberies in the Portland area. They stole cash and a watch from a streetcar conductor and postage stamps from a drugstore. They robbed butchers, saloons, and a grocery store. They spent their booty freely at night, wining and dining the ladies and gambling.

Finally the police received an anonymous tip that led them to the robbers' hideout. Detective Cordano and four others staked out the house until Tracy and Merrill showed up. Merrill arrived first, and they captured him with little trouble on February 5, 1899. The lawmen laid in wait for Tracy's arrival. Detective Weiner waited inside the house, pretending to be a friend of the Merrill family.

When Tracy arrived, Weiner kept up the role, engaging Tracy in casual conversion. So that there were no accidental deaths, Weiner suggested that he and Tracy take a walk down the block. Tracy agreed but grew suspicious as they walked farther away from the house. He jumped on a nearby train and tried to force the engineer to speed away. The engineer had seen that Tracy had jumped on the train, however, so he slowed the train to a stop. Tracy jumped off and ran, shooting all the way. Albert Way, whose father had been robbed by Tracy, shot at him and grazed Tracy's head. The wound slowed him down enough to be captured.

At the time of his arrest, Tracy was described as five feet, ten inches tall and 160 pounds, with gray eyes, light hair, and a mustache. He had a vaccine mark on his left arm and a bullet scar on his left leg. Merrill was described as five feet, eleven inches tall, with blue eyes, fair hair, and a mustache. He had four missing teeth and two vaccine marks on his left arm. The two men were convicted of assault and robbery. Merrill received a thirteen-year sentence, while Tracy received twenty years because of his earlier jailbreaks. They were sent to the Salem prison on March 22, 1899.

Since Tracy and Merrill were tried together and were partners in crime, it seems incredible that prison officials would house them in the same cell. Yet they did. Three years would pass before they could take advantage of the right set of circumstances to escape.

Someone, possibly an ex-con named Harry Wright, smuggled guns and ammunition into the prison. Supposedly, Tracy convinced Wright, who was about to be released, to acquire the weapons for him and drop them over the prison wall. From there, someone inside the wall hid the guns and ammunition in the moulding room of the prison foundry.

After Tracy and Merrill escaped from the Salem prison, they fled into the surrounding countryside. They forced a farmer named J. W. Roberts to give them some clothes so they would no longer stand out in their prison stripes. A short way down the road, they stole some horses from a barn owned by Felix Lebranch, then rode all night long. The next morning they stole a horse and buggy from Dr. P. S. White and Edward Bupease of Gervais. They headed north, toward Washington.

They were nearly recaptured in the woods near Gervais. Posses and the Oregon State National Guard were on one side and dog handlers with bloodhounds from the Washington State Penitentiary were on the other. Somehow Tracy and Merrill managed to sneak through during a moment of inattention by the posses. They arrived at the home of woodcutter August King. Tracy ordered him to fix them breakfast. King reported their appearance to local authorities as soon as they left, but they were long gone by the time the sheriff could get there. They were also seen at Needy, New Era, and Oregon City, demanding food or clothing.

When they reached the Columbia River, they had to find a way to get across. They had no money to pay to get across, so

A posse searching for Tracy and Merrill after they escaped from the Oregon State Penitentiary in Salem in 1902.
(Courtesy Jim Dullenty, Hamilton, Montana)

Tracy forced three men to row them across the river. Once on the other side, the two outlaws had a brief disagreement about which way to go next. Tracy wanted to go northeast to the Yakima country. Merrill favored going northwest to the Olympic peninsula. They ended up going straight north.

The first Washington victim of their crime spree was Mrs. Jones, whom they forced to fix them a meal. They then moved on to the home of Henry Tiede, where they helped themselves to clothes and more food before tying up Tiede and leaving. Tiede got loose quickly, however, and alerted Clark County Sheriff Marsh.

Up the road near the Salmon Creek bridge, the two desperadoes engaged in a shoot-out with hunters named Bert Biesecker and Luther Davidson. The four men spotted each other about the same time and started firing. Several shots were exchanged, and then all went quiet. The two hunters couldn't see anything and wondered if they had shot the outlaws. They waited about a half hour, then decided to return home. Just as they boarded their buggy, shots rang out again. Their horse was hit by two bullets, and Biesecker was wounded in the arm. The horse reared up and ran at full gallop all the way to Vancouver. A team of bloodhounds came out to this scene and tracked the outlaws' scent to LaCenter, where the outlaws had stolen two horses. There the country became very rough, so the posse retreated to Vancouver.

Meanwhile, the outlaws escaped north across the Lewis River and headed east of Kelso, where they found a secluded chalet. They hid out there for a week in the absence of the owner before stealing two horses and continuing.

When they reached Napavine, Tracy decided he'd had enough of Merrill. Later stories suggest that Tracy had read newspaper accounts of their exploits that gave Merrill equal credit and that Merrill was the mastermind in their exploits. Tracy felt he was really the brains behind the duo and didn't like Merrill getting any credit. He thought Merrill was a coward, always wanting to stay hidden and preferring to go hungry rather than force a meal. The two agreed to a duel, but Tracy spun around early, figuring he couldn't trust Merrill to count to ten. He was correct; Merrill was already getting ready to fire. But Tracy fired first and hit Merrill three times. Tracy dragged Merrill's body out of sight and fled.

Merrill's body wasn't found until July 14, when Mary Waggoner and her son George were out picking blackberries near the Reform School of Chehalis. Mary immediately notified Sheriff Deggeller, who conducted the investigation. He called Dan Merrill, Dave Merrill's brother, who worked at a livery stable in Chehalis, to identify the body. Though it had been some years since they had seen each other, Dan Merrill was fairly certain it was his brother.

Tracy was next seen at Bucoda, about fifteen miles south of Olympia, where he forced Ed Sanford to feed him breakfast. After that, Tracy appeared at South Bay near Olympia. On July 2, he walked into the Capital City Oyster Company and demanded that the manager, Horatio Alling, fix him a meal. Then he forced Captain A. J. Clark and his son Edwin to sail him across Puget Sound to Seattle in one of the company's gas-powered launches.

While sailing across Puget Sound, Tracy told Clark and the other deckhands how he had just killed his partner Merrill. He explained how the two had agreed to fight a duel. His stories kept the deckhands subdued; they made no attempt whatsoever to capture him. In fact, after Tracy left the boat, the deckhands told a story of a polite and gentlemanly encounter with Tracy.

Though he didn't outwardly show it, Captain Clark's nervousness caused him to drive the launch so fast that the engine overheated. Twice he had to shut it down. This was just fine with Tracy because he wanted to reach Seattle after dark. Clark reached the Seattle harbor about six o'clock at night, but it was still too light out. Tracy directed Clark to sail north and set anchor at Meadow Point, two miles north of Ballard. About six-thirty, he tied up the captain and his crew and forced deck-hand Frank Scott to row him to shore. Just as soon as Tracy was out of sight, Clark freed himself and alerted the police.

Tracy's next victims were two deputies he killed near Bothell. A posse of five men led by Deputy Sheriff Raymond followed footprints near some railroad tracks, leading them straight to Tracy. Tracy fired the deadly shots from behind a large stump. Raymond and Deputy John Williams lay dead. He also injured a reporter named Anderson. Tracy fled the scene, then stole a horse and buggy nearby. He forced the owner, Louis Johnson, to come with him.

Tracy held a gun on Johnson while he drove the buggy past Green Lake to the home of Mrs. R. H. Van Horn near Woodland Park. He forced Johnson inside the house and then made Mrs. Van Horn make him a meal. A neighbor named Butterfield was also in the house. While Tracy was there, a boy delivered some groceries to the house. Mrs. Van Horn whispered to the boy that she was being held captive by an outlaw. The boy fled the house and alerted the authorities. Instead of sending a large posse after Tracy, King County Sheriff Edward Cudihee took only two men to ambush the house. Unknown to Cudihee, Officer Frank Breece and Game Warden Neil Rawley waited for Tracy, too. A few minutes later Tracy emerged from the house with Johnson and Butterfield. Cudihee held his fire for fear of missing Tracy and hitting one of the other men. Rawley showed no such restraint. He demanded Tracy surrender. For his efforts, he and Breece were shot and killed by Tracy. Cudihee shot at Tracy as he ran, but he was wide of the mark. Once again, Tracy escaped.

Tracy next appeared at the home of August Fisher in Maple Leaf. He forced Mrs. Fisher to make him breakfast and some sandwiches to take with him. Then he took a full set of clothes and a hat and shoes. As he left he warned Mr. Fisher not to tell anyone for forty-eight hours.

Tracy headed back to Puget Sound, where he forced a Japanese fisherman to sail him to Bainbridge Island. He arrived at the home of another Johnson family and made Mrs. Johnson fix him a meal. Tracy also stole some clothes belonging to the hired man, John Anderson, as well as other items, including flour, ham, sugar, a frying pan, matches, and blankets. He tied up the family before leaving, then he forced Anderson to row him back across Puget Sound to West Seattle. Tracy dragged Anderson along with him for four days, forcing him to carry his belongings and to cook for him.

Near Renton they met May Baker, Mrs. James McKinney, and Charles Gerrells, who were out picking berries. He forced them to lead him to the Gerrellses' home a few yards away. He made Charles go into town to purchase two revolvers for him, warning him not to tell anyone or he would shoot his family. He forced Mrs. Gerrells to fix a meal for him, and he tied up Anderson so that he could not try to disarm him while he ate. Meanwhile, Charles Gerrells ignored Tracy's warning and went straight to the police.

A man came to the Gerrells' door and asked if Tracy was there. Miss Baker and Mrs. Gerrells both denied he was there while Tracy waited in the kitchen, his gun aimed at the front door. The man pretended to give up and left. Over the next two hours, crowds of lawmen surrounded the house. Tracy snuck out the back door and down a small slope toward the Cedar River. He crawled on his stomach through some tall weeds. Despite being surrounded by deputies, Tracy was able to sneak away without anyone firing a shot. In the dark, the lawmen and the newsmen may have thought Tracy was one of them.

From about July 15 to July 30, Tracy's exact whereabouts were unknown. He was supposedly spotted in Kent, Auburn, Enumclaw, Ravensdale, and some other small towns. Police kept boats patrolling up and down the Sound, ready for the next sighting. A new team of bloodhounds was brought in to sniff out the outlaw's trail. Somewhere near Covington, he was supposedly wounded by a posse, but he disappeared into a swamp. He was spotted near Black Diamond, Roslyn, and then Ellensburg. By then Tracy's exploits were being glamorized in Seattle theaters, where actors played Tracy, Merrill, Sheriff Cudihee, and various other people with whom the outlaw had come in contact.

On July 30, Tracy showed up in Wenatchee, arriving at the home of Sam McEldowney, a man Tracy had known in Portland. He forced Mrs. McEldowney to fix him lunch and dinner, and he made Sam steal some horses from his neighbor so that Tracy could ride on. Then he rode twelve miles south of town where he forced the Mottler brothers to take him across the Columbia River in their ferry. He followed Moses Coulee north, heading for Coulee City. From there, he rode east to Almira, where he camped in some caves along Wilson Creek. He stopped at the Stirrett Ranch and asked for directions to Davenport.

While traveling through the sagebrush desert, he ran across a young man named George Goldfinch. He held the young man at gunpoint, demanding that Goldfinch lead him to the nearest farm where he could hide out for a while. On August 3, Goldfinch led him to the ranch owned by brothers Eugene and Lucius Eddy, near Creston, Washington.

When he arrived, Tracy forced the Eddys to unsaddle and feed his horses, and he later made them re-shoe his horses and cut hay for them and repair his holster. Curiously, Tracy also helped them by repairing their roof. He made one of the brothers sleep with him in the haystack. After a day or two, he released George Goldfinch, believing that he would not tell the law where he was. Goldfinch returned to the Blenz farm where he worked and telegraphed Sheriff Jerry H. Gardner of Davenport.

Lawyer Maurice Smith overheard the call. He was not about to wait until the sheriff came from Davenport. He alerted Constable C. A. Straub, who immediately formed a posse that included Smith; Dr. E. C. Lanter; J. J. Morrison, a railroad section foreman; and Frank Lillengreen, a hardware store owner.

On August 5, Constable Straub arrived at the Eddy ranch about 6:30 p.m. with seventeen men. When they approached the ranch, they dismounted, leaving their horses out of sight and out of range of any gunplay. Then they crept up to a bluff overlooking the ranch to see if they could spot Tracy. Down below, Lucius Eddy was in a field mowing hay. Straub approached Eddy, asking him if he had seen Tracy. Eddy nervously replied that Tracy was there but told Straub not to let on that he was the law or else Tracy would kill him. Tracy spotted Straub and went to the barn for his gun. When he ran from the barn with his rifle, revolver, and ammunition, the posse opened fire.

Tracy first ran to a haystack, then to a big rock in the middle of the field. Tracy held off the posse for a while but realized the sinking sun shining on his rifle was giving away his position. He saw a rock nearby that would serve as a more strategic location so he darted out of his hiding spot. In that split second while he was unprotected, a bullet found him. He was struck in the leg and began bleeding profusely. He couldn't get up so he tried to drag himself through the tall grass to reach shelter.

While crawling, he was hit again in the thigh. His strength was fading fast. He always swore he'd never be taken alive. So he made the only choice possible for him. About 10:30 p.m. he took out his revolver, put it to his head, and shot himself.

The posse kept firing for a while, fooled by the grain blowing in the wind. They had heard the single shot from the revolver and guessed what it might have meant, but they didn't want to take any chances with Harry Tracy. They waited and watched all night. At daybreak, Maurice Smith and Dr. Lanter cautiously approached the rock where Tracy had last been

The Eddy Ranch, where Tracy made his final stand in 1902.
(Courtesy Jim Dullenty, Hamilton, Montana)

seen. By then, close to three hundred people had gathered at the Eddy ranch, including Sheriff Gardner and twenty-five men from Lincoln County, Sheriff Doust and twelve men from Spokane County, and King County Sheriff Cudihee. They had arrived too late to get in on the action. Harry Tracy was dead.

Sheriff Gardner arranged for the body to be taken to Davenport. Upon the arrival of the posse and the dead outlaw, the townspeople clamored to see the body and take a relic from it. By the time they were through, the body was naked. They took all his clothes and divided them up into little pieces. They took his weapons and ammunition and even cut pieces of his hair.

Tracy's body was shipped from Davenport to Seattle, and from there it was shipped south to the Salem penitentiary. Tracy was buried on the prison grounds next to his former partner Dave Merrill. Thus ended the life of a man who led the law on one of the most drawn-out chases of all time.

Shoot-Out at Kennewick

On the night of October 30, 1906, two men snuck into the Tull & Godwin General Merchandise Store and stole goods. Then they went down the street and snuck into the Kennewick Hardware Store. Soon the store was missing some of its inventory. In both places the two men wreaked havoc on the interior, breaking showcases and window fronts. Then they quietly left the area. Or did they?

The two men actually traveled less than a mile from Kennewick, the scene of the robberies. They hid in a poplar grove near the Burlington Northern railroad bridge that spanned the Columbia River. This area was a known hangout for transients. Unknown to the two men, they had been seen by Mrs. R. H. Anderson and an alarm had already been sounded. Kennewick Marshal Mike Glover and storeowner Mr. Godwin began an immediate search of the area along the railroad tracks up to the railroad bridge. But somehow they overlooked the spot where the bandits were hiding.

The robbers were warming themselves around a fire when two men approached them. Deputy Joe Holzhey and H. E. Roseman, proprietor of the Stag Saloon, had been searching for the stolen items when they found some blankets in a nearby haystack. They saw the two men huddled around the fire and decided to ask them if they knew anything. Before they could say anything, one of the robbers said that they didn't appreciate being watched and if Holzhey and Roseman didn't go away there would be trouble. Holzhey replied that they were simply looking for stolen goods and asked the men if they knew anything about the robberies. They denied knowing anything about them. Holzhey briefly looked through their possessions before he and Roseman headed back toward town. The two crooks breathed more easily for a minute.

But Holzhey wasn't through with his investigation. The proximity of the stolen blankets to the two men by the railroad tracks and their strange statement about wanting to be left alone made him suspicious. When he and Roseman got back to town, they met Sheriff Alex G. McNeill and Marshal Glover. Holzhey told them about the two men, and the four decided to head back to the poplar grove.

The robbers saw them coming, and the same man who warned Holzhey and Roseman before warned them again, saying, "Good evening, gentlemen, you are looking for trouble and you'll get it." McNeill tried to explain that they were officers, but it was too late. One bandit shot Holzhey and killed Glover with a rifle. Then he fired at McNeill, wounding him in the hand and in the stomach. It was dark, so McNeill could not see clearly. He fired in the direction of the shots he heard and managed to shoot one of the outlaws. The other desperado fired a few random shots, and then fled on foot.

Roseman helped McNeill board a railroad speeder that stood nearby. They rode it back to town to spread the word. A posse quickly assembled and rode the speeder back downriver to try to stop the outlaw from escaping. The sheriff's office sent a team of riders to guard the Kiona area, about halfway between Kennewick and Prosser. Another team searched nearby Currant Island. Other teams scouted up the Columbia River. Deputies guarded the railroad bridge to make sure the outlaw didn't try to sneak across. Pasco police watched the other side. All the precautions were unnecessary. The outlaw had never gone far from the scene of the original shooting. He hid in a ditch near the poplar grove. At about eleven o'clock, a posse found him there. Unfortunately, before he could be captured, another tragedy befell the town. Forrest Perry, a volunteer, approached the ditch and demanded that the outlaw give himself up. Another volunteer, seeing only Perry's shadowy figure, thought he was the suspect. He shot at him and killed him. Finally, the outlaw, who turned out to be a man named Robert A. "Kid" Barker, surrendered. Marshal Owens handcuffed him, and Barker did not argue or fight.

An angry armed mob watched as Owens took Barker to the jail in Prosser, the county seat. Barker told officers that the dead robber's name was Jake Lake, a thirty-five-year-old sheepherder from Wallula. He had only known Lake for a day, having just met him the day before.

Kid Barker hailed from Florence, Colorado. He was only about eighteen years old. He admitted to shooting at the sheriff, saying that he only fired because he was afraid that Lake would kill him if he didn't. He denied any involvement in the robberies of the two stores. Police were skeptical since innocent men usually did not carry the sort of weapons that these men carried nor did they shoot at lawmen unprovoked. However, the lawmen did not find any of the stolen goods in the bandits' camp.

Judge C. G. Baker presided over a preliminary hearing on November 7. Barker was charged with the first-degree murder of Marshal Glover. He pled not guilty, stating that he had shot at the sheriff but not at Glover. Six witnesses were called at the hearing, including Mrs. Joshua Swindler, who lived in a tent near the scene of the shooting. She testified that she heard

Barker say, as he ran from the scene, that he would "kill all of the sons of bitches yet." Other witnesses said they saw Barker firing in the direction of Glover, but none could say for sure that he shot him. He was bound over for trial and held without bail. He did not have an attorney.

While Kid Barker waited in jail, Marshal Owens wrote to Barker's father to tell him what had happened. Mr. Barker was living in Grangeville, Idaho, where he had been prospecting. He came to see his son a few days after the hearing. Both were very upset and broke down in tears. The father was very poor but said he would do everything he could for his young son. Mr. Barker stated that if his son was guilty he should be punished. Their prisoner was despondent, and officers were afraid he might try suicide. As the trial drew closer, Mr. Barker managed to raise enough money to hire a lawyer named Lon Boyle. Boyle also retained the Honorable H. J. Snively of North Yakima to assist him. The arraignment was scheduled for January 15, 1907.

Before he could face trial and a certain prison sentence, Barker escaped from the Prosser jail on January 9. At about eight o'clock that night, Barker and four other men overpowered the jailer, C. F. Gilpin. During the day inmates were allowed access to the corridors. But at night, Gilpin locked the prisoners into their individual cells. When Gilpin ordered the men to go into their cells, two of the men complied, but Barker and a man named R. C. Bear threw a blanket over a table and hid under it. Gilpin didn't see them and thought they had already gone into their cells. When he opened the door to the corridor, Barker and Bear jumped him. They took his gun, his keys, and his money then gagged him with a towel and tied him up. Then Barker,

Bear, George Simpson, a forger, and Fred Thomas, a horse thief, ran from the jail. As he ran out the door, Barker exclaimed that he would kill anyone who tried to stop him.

Soon after the escape, Gilpin managed to work off the gag and began yelling for the authorities. F. A. Jenne was walking behind the courthouse and heard him, but Jenne couldn't get inside the jail since Barker had locked it. Gilpin yelled to him from inside and explained what had happened. Jenne called Sheriff McNeill, and on his way to the jail, McNeill ran right into Thomas. Thomas tried to explain that he was on his way to the sheriff's house to tell him of the jailbreak, but McNeill didn't believe him. He marched him back to the jail and turned him over to Marshal Winters. A short time later, McNeill found Simpson, who was still carrying the jail keys.

McNeill immediately organized a posse and sent men to seal off the town. More than fifty men surrounded the rail yards. He also sent a telegraph to Harry Draper in Spokane, asking him to bring his bloodhounds.

Barker and Bear were still at large at six o'clock the next morning when Draper arrived with his bloodhounds. The dogs were set on the trail immediately, but they couldn't pick up the scent. Most people figured Barker and Bear couldn't have gone far on foot, but it seemed that they had. The posse got their first lead about lunch time, when a conductor on a westbound train at Byron, about five miles west, said he'd seen two suspicious-looking characters hanging around. He did not see them board the train. McNeill sent some men to check out the lead, but they found nothing.

Most thought Barker and Bear would head toward the Horse Heaven Hills, where Bear had stolen some horses. He knew the country there and could steal more horses. Barker didn't know the country, so it was assumed he would follow Bear. It soon became obvious that these assumptions were wrong.

Bear stopped at O. Jeru's house to ask about Clement Mosier, a man he had worked for before. Jeru told him that Mosier was working in Sunnyside, so Bear headed there. As soon as they heard this news, two men, Hal Jack and C. S. Cady, trailed Bear to Sunnyside. By the time they arrived, Bear had already turned himself in. Bear claimed he didn't know where Barker had gone.

Meanwhile, Barker had breakfast at A. B. Richmond's house in the Horse Heaven Hills. Three men rode to Richmond's place ready to arrest Barker, but he left the house before anyone could catch him. Two days later the three men returned after covering 175 miles without finding a trace of Barker. They followed the Columbia River for about thirty miles but found no clues. The river was so choked with ice that they felt no one could row across, and they presumed that Barker was still on the west side of the river.

McNeill always believed Barker would be recaptured. He thought that Barker would hide in the Horse Heaven Hills until the weather got better and the lawmen stopped looking for him. But posses covered the area all around Kiona and both sides of the Yakima River. They searched the Yakima Valley from Prosser to Sunnyside. They checked all the train stations and were sure he did not escape by train. There was speculation that he would head to Portland, since he had friends there. But Barker was never found, and the case remains unsolved.

Peter Miller

On Thanksgiving Day in 1908, Hugh McMahon, manager of The American Bar in Seattle, locked up for the night and started for home, down Pike Street to the streetcar stop on Fourth Street. After a short ride, he continued on foot to Aloha Street, where he lived. He was nearly home when he was accosted by three men. One of the men had a beard and wore a derby. He was about five feet, nine inches tall and about thirty-five years old.

The three men pushed McMahon down and knocked him over the head with a sand-filled rubber hose. They ripped off his tie to remove his diamond stickpin, slid the diamond ring off his finger, and stole a Swiss pocketwatch he was keeping for a friend. In total these items were worth about $700. They rifled through his vest pockets and stole several hundred dollars in cash, then tossed McMahon's body over a barbed wire fence. The next day one of the robbers traveled to Spokane and sold the diamonds to a pawn shop called Ferrin & Jackman.

Early the next morning. McMahon's body was discovered by Tom Davis, who was on his way to work. McMahon's Great Dane, Nell, had come to stand guard over McMahon's body, and Davis recognized the dog. He hurried to his office and called the police. By the time Captain Charles Tennant arrived, McMahon's wife had arrived at the scene and positively identified her husband.

Tennant talked to several witnesses, including J. W. Coleman, who said he had talked to McMahon on the streetcar the night before, and a waitress named Ellen Davis, who saw a bearded man with a dark hat and a turned-up collar hanging around the lot where McMahon's body was found. Several other witnesses remembered that McMahon was wearing his jewelry that day. Mrs. Atkinson and Mr. Van Stone, who boarded at the property next door to the murder scene, said they had heard a scuffle outside the previous night. They also said they had heard someone cry out. Charles T. McDonald, a milkman, said he saw the body as he made his early-morning deliveries.

Coroner F. M. Carroll took the body downtown, while Tennant looked around for clues. He used a skeleton key to enter the vacant house that stood on the lot where McMahon's body was found. There were no footprints in the dust, but he did find a piece of a burned match and the stub of a cigar. He kept the two small pieces of evidence. He surmised that the killer had waited inside the house until his victim walked by. He figured that the perpetrator must have known that McMahon was wearing some valuable items.

Who did this dastardly deed? Investigations would later reveal that it was a man named Peter Miller and his two henchmen, Charles Rose and George Smith. Miller was born in Germantown, Pennsylvania, in 1873. The death of Miller's father at an early age precipitated his move to Italy. Miller spent most of his formative years in Europe.

At age sixteen, he attended the University of Berlin. He graduated from there and went on to study criminal jurisprudence in Turin, Italy. He also studied at the University of Paris and the University of Vienna and received an MD from the University of Bologna and a PhD from the University of Vienna. After college, he served as a surgeon in the Boer War in South Africa. When he was discharged, he returned to the United States and toured the New England states, lecturing on sociology subjects.

How did such a well-educated and sophisticated man end up on the wrong side of the law? Throughout his entire ordeal, Miller would claim that he never robbed or killed anyone. He would claim that the stolen items found in his possession were given to him by someone else. But the evidence stacked up against him.

The dust was hardly settled on the McMahon case before Miller struck again. He called Frank Atwood, owner of the Globe Art Company, to talk to him about some property that Atwood was selling. They made arrangements to meet on a Saturday. Miller called Atwood again the day before they were to meet, telling Atwood that he had sprained his ankle and could not meet him at the property. He asked Atwood to come to his house instead, to talk about the deal. When Atwood arrived at Miller's home, Miller pretended to be a man sent by the man who had originally phoned Atwood. He spoke very proper English with a foreign accent. He wore a derby and sported a small mustache. He escorted Atwood to a home nearby.

Atwood didn't suspect anything until he entered the home and discovered it completely unfurnished. This seemed odd to him, but before he could ask a question, Miller hit him from behind. Atwood collapsed to the ground, and when he turned around, Miller swung a heavy tool at him. Atwood deflected the blow with his arm. The two struggled for a few minutes. Miller's fake beard and mustache fell off, and Miller presumed Atwood had seen enough of his face that he could identify him to the police. Now he had to kill him. Atwood quickly realized that Miller might have murder on his mind. He struggled from the floor and ran away as fast as he could. Miller shot at him and wounded him in the knee and grazed the back of his head, but adrenaline kept Atwood running until he reached a nearby house, where he phoned the police.

By the time the police arrived, Miller was gone. Captain Tennant was one of the first men on the scene. He searched the empty house and found three more cigar stubs and several matches. Because of these clues, he figured the same man who had killed McMahon had attacked Atwood. Tennant also found the fake mustache and beard that had fallen off the assailant during the struggle.

The two incidents were just the first in a long series of robberies and deaths around greater Seattle. Most of them occurred in wealthy neighborhoods and to wealthy men. Right after the Atwood assault, Miller robbed and killed Mike Conway, owner of a saloon. Just like in the McMahon case, Miller waited until Conway was on his way home before he attacked. He carefully studied the man's habits before deciding how and when to get the man's diamond jewelry. Miller and another man hid about a block from Conway's home before they jumped him.

Many of the robberies took place when the victims were less than a block from their homes. Those who wore diamond rings and stickpins were Miller's main targets. When the trend was noticed, some men stopped wearing their fine jewelry, hoping to thwart the robbers.

Tennant soon began to believe that the robber/murderer was a part of the circles traveled by Seattle's rich men. The robber seemed to know where all the other rich men lived and what their habits were. Tennant started spending some time in gentlemen's clubs around the city, hoping to pick up a lead. He saw and spoke to Peter Miller several times in these clubs before he knew he was involved in the crimes. One day the two men were talking about the McMahon death when Miller offered to buy Tennant a drink. Tennant declined but said that he wouldn't mind having a cigar. Miller gave him one called an El Rio Rey, a special imported cigar. Tennant thanked him for it, then left without smoking it.

Though he didn't really suspect Miller at the time, he gave the cigar to a cigar maker to analyze the contents. He had already given the man several other samples to try to match against the cigar stubs he had taken from the two murder scenes. None had matched. But this time he hit the jackpot. Miller's cigar had the same type of filler as the other two samples, and the cigar maker declared that it was very rare to find that type in Seattle. Tennant knew he was on to something, so he sent two of his best detectives, Lee Barbee and Frank Kennedy, to follow Miller.

A few days after talking to Tennant, Miller struck again. This time he attacked a man named Ace Hamilton, who was sporting a large diamond ring when he was robbed. He had just left a card game at one of the clubs that Tennant had visited. Tennant was quickly called to the scene. When asked if he had talked to Miller lately, Hamilton replied that he had. Miller had asked him where he lived and how he got home. Miller had warned him about thieves. Hamilton thought Miller had just been concerned for his safety.

Even though the description didn't match, Tennant felt he had his man. He asked Barbee and Kennedy if they had learned anything. Barbee said on the night of the robbery, he had followed Miller to his hotel and saw him go in. He watched the building the entire night, and Miller did not leave. The only man he saw leave was taller than Miller and wore a black beard and mustache. Barbee didn't know that Hamilton had also described such a man. Tennant told Barbee to keep an eye on every black-bearded man who left the hotel.

By that time, Miller had teamed up with Willis Taylor. Taylor was a small-time hood and only about sixteen years old. On April 26, 1909, the two met outside the mansion of Fred Fischer, a prosperous merchant on Capitol Hill. Taylor was smaller, so he broke a bathroom window and squeezed through, then let Miller in through the front door. They looked around for likely objects to steal and came across a very valuable silver table service, a purse containing $20 in gold, a pair of silver military hair brushes, and a silver coffee urn. They also helped themselves to Fischer's expensive cigars and whiskey.

Miller and Taylor had a very busy weekend indeed. They also robbed S. H. Grattan on Melrose Avenue, taking two gold rings, a gold alarm clock, and a pearl necklace. Matt Lutz on East Prospect Street was relieved of six dozen pieces of silverware and a suitcase. R. E. Gardner was robbed of two suitcases and some other articles. Lena Champagne reported that her gold watch was stolen, and T. J. Hyde, Gus Brown, and J. A. Morrison also reported being burglarized. All these robberies occurred in one weekend! Later, most were attributed to Miller. Only one man targeted by Miller escaped with his valuables intact.

Miller met a Mr. Mansfield when he went to Spokane to pawn McMahon's diamonds. Miller and George Smith planned to go to Mansfield's office and to pretend that they were interested in having their fortunes told by Mansfield. As soon as Mansfield went into his routine, they would jump him for the $10,000 he supposedly kept in his underwear. Unfortunately, the plot didn't go as planned. Mansfield put up a fight and forced Miller through a glass partition. Miller escaped, but Smith was fined $100 for assault. Several weeks later, Miller spotted Mansfield walking down a Seattle street. He followed him for quite a while, but never found a good opportunity to rob him.

A few nights after the robbery spree, Tennant ran into Miller at the same club where he had seen him before. Miller was smoking a cigar. Tennant casually mentioned what a good cigar it was that Miller had given him on the earlier occasion. He asked if he had another, and Miller gave him one. He said it wasn't the same El Rio Rey, but it was just as good. It happened to be the same brand that was stolen out of Fischer's home.

Evidently Miller didn't suspect that he was under surveillance because on May 17 he and Taylor paid another visit to the Fischer home. Apparently they had discovered that the silver set they had stolen was incomplete. Miller's fence told him he would not take it unless it was a complete set. So Miller and Taylor went back to get the rest. They broke into the house just as easily as they had before, and they were in and out before anyone could discover them. They didn't leave anything behind to tie them to the killings or the other robberies, but Tennant still thought they were all related.

Not one to lay low for long, Miller struck again on June 21. This time the victim was a man named Marcellus H. Young. Miller and Taylor staked out the house until Young left. Once again, young Taylor broke a small window and crawled through. Then he let Miller into the house. They spent more than two hours ransacking the house and stealing anything they could carry, including furs, silver, clothes, and money.

The day after the Young burglary, Barbee and Kennedy followed Taylor to a house on Terry Avenue. Tennant swore out an arrest warrant and told the detectives to arrest anyone in the house for burglary. Miller and Taylor were both in the house when the detectives arrived. The pair feigned outrage, and Miller demanded to know why he was under arrest. The detectives told him he was wanted for the Marcellus Young burglary. He just laughed.

After the detectives took Miller to the city jail, they went back to search the house. They found many of the items from Young's house there. When asked to explain how they got there, Miller said that Taylor had brought those items to the house without his knowledge. Taylor went along with Miller's story, but he claimed the items belonged to his father. Despite their claims of innocence, both were held without bail until trial. The burglaries of Seattle's rich stopped as soon as Miller was in jail.

Tennant got a big break while he was interviewing a convict named Buck Martin at the state penitentiary in Salem, Oregon. Martin had once known Miller. He said that Miller and two other men named Charles Rose and George Smith had killed McMahon. Martin said that Miller often went by the name Big Pete and that he frequently wore a black beard and mustache as a disguise and put inserts in his shoes to appear taller.

Martin also mentioned the little black book that Miller carried. Martin said the book contained a list of all the important men in the city, their addresses, their schedules, and the routes they traveled. It also listed the types of valuables the men had.

At the time Martin mentioned the black book to Tennant, no one knew that Tennant had confiscated such a book from Miller. Tennant knew Martin had to be telling the truth. Martin's testimony would help seal the lid on Miller's conviction.

Before the trial, Taylor confessed to his attorney, T. D. Page, that he had participated in both the Fischer and Young burglaries with Miller. Miller broke down and admitted to the crimes also. Miller figured getting tried on the burglary charge would be better than being tried on a murder rap. But then he found out about Washington's habitual criminal law. If he admitted to committing the two burglaries, it would only take one more crime to put him in prison for life. And he did have one more felony, committed out of state. It would be a trial for his life.

The trial began October 28, 1909. Miller represented himself and argued very eloquently on his own behalf. He asked many intelligent questions when impaneling the jury. He objected to the state's witnesses being allowed in the courtroom since all of his witnesses were not present. The judge agreed this was unfair and excused the witnesses from the courtroom.

But testimony by Young and Taylor ensured he would be convicted. Young testified to the items that had been stolen from his house. Taylor described how he and Miller had robbed Young's house.

Miller's defense consisted mostly of testimony regarding the cruel treatment of the jail inmates by the lawmen and how such treatment forced him into a confession. He got the charge dropped from first-degree burglary to second-degree burglary. This was only reasonable, since the charge of first-degree burglary required the building's occupants to be home at the time of the burglary. Miller tried to win sympathy from the jury by claiming that he suffered from tuberculosis and that jail time would only aggravate his condition.

The jury took only three hours to come back with a verdict of guilty. The charge carried a penalty of six months to fifteen years in prison. Miller immediately appealed the case to the state supreme court, claiming that his confession was given under duress so it was not admissible in court. He also claimed that he was subjected to cruelty in the "dark hole" and repeatedly threatened. He said his case was prejudiced by the fact that nine of the twelve jurors who convicted him were the same ones who convicted two other criminals earlier in October. The supreme court granted him a new trial, but he was convicted again.

Then he was sent to Pierce County to be tried on the Fischer burglary charge. Mrs. Fischer told how about a month before the first burglary, a man came to her house and asked about a specific house number. There was no such house number on that street. She was certain that Miller was that man. Other witnesses testified about the articles taken from the house on Terry Street, including burglars' tools. During the trial Miller lied on the stand about his previous felony convictions. He never revealed that he had served time in a New York prison and Joliet Prison in Illinois. By perjuring himself in court, he committed a third felony. Miller was found guilty of the Fischer burglaries and sentenced to life in prison as a habitual criminal.

Miller appealed this case, too. Again he based it on the improper confession. Again the decision was reversed. He won a new trial but was convicted again. He tried to appeal based on the fact that during the second trial, his right to a speedy trial had not been observed. This time he was denied an appeal, with the reasoning that the speedy trial rule only applies in the original trial.

Peter Miller took his case to the supreme court of Washington seven times, but in 1913 he finally started serving his sentence. He was never tried for the murder of Hugh McMahon or Mike Conway, the assault on Atwood, or any of the other robberies. His education stood him in good stead, and he was soon put in charge of the prison library. With contributions, he built up the library from a few hundred to several thousand books. When he was paroled twenty-five years later, he went to live with his brother in Mexico. He died there about 1940.

Lum You

During the western gold rush, many Chinese laborers came to the United States to take advantage of the economic prosperity. Many of them labored at mines owned by others; some worked claims that white men had abandoned because they felt they could no longer make a profit. The gold rush caused towns to spring up all over the West, and it wasn't long before a faster method of transportation and communication was needed. Along came the railroad. Chinese laborers went to work on the railroad and were, in fact, in demand because they worked harder and for less money than other men.

Eventually, though, the railroads were completed, and Chinese labor was no longer as welcome as it once had been. In fact, many felt the Chinese were taking jobs from American citizens. Because of the resentment, people easily believed that a Chinese worker accused of a crime was guilty, even if he had been provoked into it. Such was the case of Lum You.

Lum You worked in the Willapa Bay area on the Washington coast. Lum You and his fellow countrymen fished, gathered oysters, worked in canneries, and tended the many cranberry bogs in the area. Some men also worked for farmers, clearing land and digging ditches. Lum You was a little different from those around him. He was a proud man who dressed nicely and carried a large gold watch on a chain. Sometimes he wove silk strands into his braid.

Lum You lived at the China House at the Chabot cranberry bogs at Bay Center, at the tip of a small peninsula in Pacific County. His position was similar to that of a union foreman.

He acted as an intermediary between the workers and the employers. Most thought him a friendly and peaceable man, unless pushed. Children liked him because he would play games with them and tell them stories. There were sometimes disagreements within the Chinese community, but County Sheriff Chester Egbert generally let them settle their own differences.

The first sign of trouble came not long after Lum You moved into the area. About June 28, 1894, Lum You entered the cabin of Joe Ging in Bruceport. The two had had a disagreement over money. Ging had sold a gun for Lum You for $1.50. Evidently Lum You thought that the gun was worth more than that. He went to South Bend, the county seat, to have Ging arrested for assault, though what might have occurred to justify this charge is unknown. As usual, Egbert wasn't interested in disputes among the Chinese. Furthermore, he wouldn't arrest Ging unless Lum You agreed to pay the court costs.

So Lum You took matters into his own hands. He walked to Ging's cabin to teach him a lesson. While the man slept, Lum You struck him with an ax just over the left eye. Then he fled from the cabin and headed toward South Bend. Another man, Lee Ging, lay in a nearby cot.

Dave Hill and Doc Riddell heard the cries of Ging and saw Lum You fleeing the area. They caught him and took him to South Bend.

Dr. Gruwell tended the injured Ging. The ax had left a three-inch gash over his left eye. A portion of the man's skull was crushed and a small piece of bone had to be removed. Gruwell successfully operated on Ging in South Bend.

Lum You was held in the county jail on the charge of assault with intent to kill. The sheriff held the three men who lived with Ging on $75 bonds as witnesses.

At the trial, Lee Ging testified that he had been smoking opium and was not really paying attention when he heard the thump of Lum You's ax hitting the ceiling while swinging it toward his victim. He was not able to stop Lum You from hitting Joe Ging, but had wrested the ax away from him afterward, he said. The other two residents of the cabin were not present when the assault took place and could only say they saw Lum You running away. Joe Ging, his head in a bandage, took the stand. He said that he had been asleep when he was hit and didn't really know who had done it. He had passed out and the next thing he knew the doctor was there.

The defense argued that Lum You had tried to get relief legally for the assault committed on him and that the county attorney had denied him justice. It was only natural, said the defense, that he took matters into his own hands. Lum You pled not guilty, though he did admit to assaulting Joe Ging. He still felt himself justified. He was sentenced to six months in jail and a $500 fine.

After he served his sentence, Lum You went back to work at Bay Center. He lived a trouble-free, if backbreaking, life in the cranberry bogs and oyster farms for several years. But in 1901, trouble came to haunt him once again. August 6, 1901, began like any other day. A fisherman and oyster harvester named Oscar Bloom bumped into Lum You in the street, seemingly on purpose. Lum You was annoyed but let it go. At about nine o'clock that night, Lum You played cards in the local saloon. Bloom bumped into him again, knocking the cards out of his hand. Bloom appeared to have been drinking. He grabbed Lum You around the neck and stole his valuables from him.

Lum You knew complaining to Egbert would be useless, so he went back to his room to retrieve a gun he had there. Bloom also left for his home. Lum You reached his place first. He retrieved his gun then headed out onto the street. Passing a neighbor's house, he warned a young boy to stay out of the way so that he wouldn't get shot. Bloom was standing on his porch hunting for his keys when Lum You caught up with him. Before Bloom could step into his house, Lum You shot him. Then he ran from the scene. Bloom staggered into his home and collapsed into bed. Many heard the shot, but no one went to Bloom's aid.

Bloom's absence was noted the next day. Egbert, Dr. Gruwell, and the county prosecutor rode the steamer down the Willapa River out into Willapa Bay to Bay Center to hunt for Bloom. Accompanied by L. L. Bush, a notary public, they found Bloom at his home, mortally wounded in the stomach from a gunshot. He was not yet dead and was able to tell the lawmen what had happened. He said he had meant no harm in his teasing of Lum You. He said that Lum You had broken into his home and shot him. There were signs of forced entry, so Bloom's version seemed to tell the true story. Bloom died later in the day. The coroner would find that the bullet had passed through his bladder and intestines and lodged in his spinal column

When the citizens found out what had happened, most were on Lum You's side, knowing the type of man Bloom was. But some of the companies that employed the Chinese in the area insisted that Lum You be prosecuted for daring to shoot a white man. At the time, he was not particularly popular among his own people either. The *South Bend Journal* reported that, "though he has a rather repulsive face, he walks with a strut and has a good opinion of himself."

A short while later, Sheriff Thomas Roney arrested Lum You. Sheriff Roney escorted him back to South Bend on the steamer. On the journey, Lum You told the sheriff how Bloom had been annoying him. He told him that Bloom had taken $40.75 from him and that Bloom left the store first and was still standing on his porch when he shot him.

The trial began on October 8, 1901. W. H. Gudgel represented Lum You. Some facts of the case were not disputed, including the fact that Lum You had shot Bloom. The question was whether he was justified or provoked into the murder. The gun that Lum You used was introduced as evidence, as was Bloom's dying statement. The two doctors who performed the autopsy testified as to the wounds sustained by Bloom and his manner of death.

But there was a good deal of conflicting testimony over whether or not Lum You actually entered Bloom's home, and there was doubt about whether or not Bloom had robbed Lum You. Some who knew Bloom said he was not drunk that night, as Lum You insisted that he was. Others said that Bloom teased everyone and was not singling out Lum You. The prosecution tried to make a case of Lum You's occasionally volatile temper as evidenced by the Ging incident.

Through an interpreter and his own heavily accented English, Lum You testified on his own behalf. Again he insisted that Bloom had started calling him names and taunting him.

He said that he had heard that Bloom had threatened him earlier in the year. He related how Bloom had wrestled with him and stolen the money that he had on him. He admitted to shooting Bloom but said that he had been provoked, just as he had testified in his previous trial.

The jury leaned heavily in Lum You's favor, but one man held out. After two hours, the others grew tired of arguing, so they gave in since the verdict had to be unanimous. Unfortunately, the jury's lethargy spelled the death penalty for Lum You. They had given in to the dissenting juror because they thought that Lum You would receive a light sentence. Instead, he was sentenced to be hanged.

Gudgel immediately motioned for a new trial, arguing that the sentence was excessively harsh and that the jury was influenced by the fact that Lum You was Chinese. He said that Lum You should only have been found guilty of second-degree murder. Judge Rice denied the motion. Lum You was sentenced to hang on January 31, 1902. The sheriff's office was deluged with requests to attend the hanging.

Lum You was despondent over the verdict. Due to the language barrier, he had not immediately understood the seriousness of what was happening to him. When everything about the sentencing was explained to him, Lum You finally realized he would pay the ultimate penalty. His despair led him to a daring escape from the jail on January 14, 1902.

At about half past one that afternoon, P. D. Larson, A. B. Griffith, C. J. Griffith, and Jess West went to the jail to see Lum You. Deputy Markham took the men back to the cell, but to the surprise of all the men, Lum You was not there. The deputy quickly looked throughout the jail, but Lum

You was nowhere to be found. Outside the jail, footprints leading toward the river were the only clue to the direction he took.

Lum You's escape has never been satisfactorily explained. No bars were cut, and no other marks were found anywhere. Some people thought that someone may have purposely left his cell door unlocked. Another theory is that someone made a wax impression of the lock and made a key from it. Whatever the truth, there was no doubt that Lum You had escaped. The newspaper office printed wanted posters and distributed them throughout the county. Posses roamed the woods, and county commissioners offered a reward of $200 for his recapture.

Lum You never left the area. He hid in the woods not far from town. He had just built a fire to keep warm when Will Peters and Ab Stevens stumbled upon him in the woods. Lum

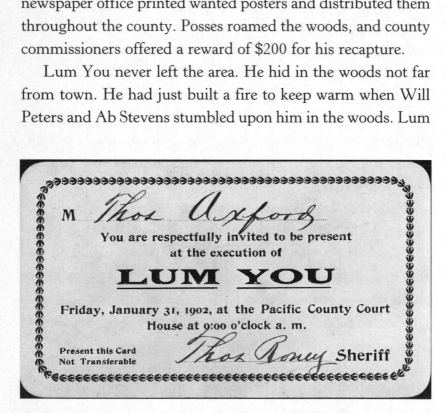

Sample of invitation issued by Sheriff Roney to attend the hanging of Lum You.
(Collection of Pacific County Historical Society. PCHS #6–27–81–1)

You ran toward the home of Frank Dodge, where he grabbed a rifle, but it wouldn't fire. Dodge and two others saw him run over the next hill.

Two days later, Lum You was recaptured. About eight o'clock in the morning, some men found some muddy footprints on a road that led past Herman Martin's house. They followed the footprints to Lum You, hiding behind a log about twenty feet from the road. He did not resist arrest. He wore an overcoat that he had stolen or received from someone since his escape. He carried a broken knife and $7 in change. He also had a half-gallon bucket with some bread, meat, and a bottle of whiskey. He swallowed the entire contents of the bottle when he was captured, then he begged the men to shoot him or hang him on the spot. By the time the men returned him to the jail cell, he was too drunk to walk or talk intelligibly.

The execution proceeded on the date it was originally scheduled. The county did not have a gallows, so one was jerry-rigged in the old courthouse in South Bend. A pulley mechanism was rigged over a ventilator opening in the floor. An elaborate arrangement of ropes was built so that the four men pulling on them would not know which one of them actually sprang the trap. The sheriff issued an incredible five hundred invitations to witness the hanging. Many of them were kept as souvenirs.

Sheriff Roney and W. H. Cornelius escorted Lum You to the gallows. He calmly said goodbye to the crowd. At 9:15 a.m., Roney struck a gong three times. A few seconds later, the trap was sprung and Lum You dropped through, dying a few seconds later. He was cut down and placed in a cheap pine box. Deputy Z. B. Brown donated a small area near the road on his own property for Lum You's burial so that his friends could visit the grave.

Lum You's execution was the first and only one ever held in Pacific County. All subsequent executions took place at the state prison in Walla Walla. The site of the first courthouse in South Bend is now referred to as Hangman's Park.

William Frederick Jahns

On October 27, 1909, William Frederick Jahns prepared for a trip to Chicago. He and his housekeeper, Agnes Jansen, planned to leave his farm at Cedonia, Washington, and drive to Blue Creek, where they would catch a connecting train to Spokane. At least, that's what Jahns told all his friends. He actually had something else in mind.

Jahns's two hired hands, George Hilton and Jack Tisth, helped pack the wagon for the trip. Agnes Jansen prepared some food to eat while they were on the road. At midnight, Jahns drove the wagon down the road. But instead of heading northeast toward Blue Creek, he actually turned southeast. Jansen, not being familiar with the area, didn't notice that Jahns wasn't traveling in the right direction. Occasionally the two talked about their future plans. Jahns and Jansen were both German immigrants, and Jahns had told people he and Agnes were going to Chicago to recruit other Germans to settle a colony near Cedonia. He had bought land for the purpose.

At three in the morning, Jahns arrived at the Hergesheimer property and suggested that they stop for the night since he wasn't sure where he was. He surmised that in daylight he could get them back on the right track. Jansen agreed. Since the house was unoccupied, no one would object to them trespassing on the property. Jahns jumped down from the wagon to open the gate and directed Jansen to drive the team through. As she did so, Jahns pulled out a gun. Before she could react, he shot and killed her. He jumped up on the wagon and drove it over to some logs that he had piled up earlier. He placed her

Outlaw Tales of Washington

body on the heap and lit it on fire. Several hours later, there was nothing left of Agnes Jansen.

What could have possessed Jahns to commit such a horrible crime? A study of Jahns's past reveals that he may have been motivated by greed. Or perhaps he was just insane. He was born in Germany in 1848, but he left there at the age of nineteen to avoid being drafted into the German army. He first settled in Pennsylvania, where he adopted the name Frank Romandorf to keep the army from finding him. He worked for a railroad before moving to Rio de Janeiro. He traveled around the world to South Africa, Hong Kong, Australia, and Asia Minor, apparently thinking that the German army was coming after him. He eventually came back to the United States and settled in Nebraska, where he worked as a farmer. Somewhere along the line he got married. From Nebraska, he moved on to Wyoming, where he lived only a short time.

Sometime in the winter of 1903 or 1904, Jahns, still known as Romandorf, showed up in Maple Falls, northeast of Bellingham, Washington. He bought some property next to James Logan. Both properties were on the Nooksack River. Jahns's son Ed and Ed's family joined him a few months later. Ed worked for a while as a butcher then later bought the butcher shop.

Then people started disappearing. Romandorf hired Fred Helms in 1905, and one day, Helms left and never came back. The following summer, Romandorf hired Jack Green. Green told the sheriff that he intended to file charges of attempted murder against Ed for pushing him against a saw. Green went to talk to Romandorf about the incident and was never seen again.

Then one fall night in 1906, both Romandorf and Logan disappeared after a severe storm. Logan had last been seen leaving a store with some purchases bundled up in a sack. At first neighbors thought the two missing men might have died during the storm. But a few days later, a neighbor was looking around Logan's property and found Logan's horse dead from a gunshot. The neighbors began to suspect foul play.

Sheriff Andrew Williams of Bellingham investigated the crime. Soon after the disappearance, he heard from G. M. Strickfadden, postmaster of Maple Falls. On November 15, Strickfadden had received a letter from Logan that was postmarked in Seattle. The letter instructed the postmaster to forward Logan's mail to Hoboken, New Jersey. Strickfadden doubted that the handwriting was Logan's, but he couldn't prove that it wasn't. A short while later, Logan's property was sold to a man named Frank Rankins. The title transfer was filed in Whatcom County, and Rankins paid $5,000 cash for the farm. Evidence seemed to support that Logan was alive. Was Romandorf alive too?

Three months after Romandorf disappeared, his son Ed got in trouble for selling a mortgaged horse. The charge was settled out of court, but Ed left Maple Falls soon after and joined his father in the small town of Cedonia, Washington, a few miles from the Columbia River in Stevens County. Earlier in the year, Romandorf had purchased property in Cedonia and changed his name to James Logan, the name of the man he had killed in Maple Falls. He hired his son and another man to help work the farm. Over the next year and a half, Logan bought more land around his property and organized the Cascade Land and Cattle Company.

During that time he met D. R. Shively, a landowner in Addy, about fifteen miles away from Cedonia. After several discussions, Jahns, now posing as Logan, told Shively he could get him a good deal on his land. In February 1908, he made the arrangements to sell Shively's land.

On March 1, Shively drove to Spokane to meet Jahns and close the land deal. In a quiet hotel room, Jahns slipped deadly drugs into Shively's drink. After Shively died, Jahns dumped his body in a trunk and shipped the trunk to his ranch at Cedonia. He instructed one of his hands to bury the trunk, without telling him its contents. As instructed, the hired man buried the trunk on Jahns's property behind the house. He never looked inside it.

On March 6, the land transaction was complete. George A. Herman of Chicago bought Shively's property for $6,000. Three or four months later Herman sold the property to a James Monaghan of Spokane. Both names were fictitious, made up by Jahns so that he could later transfer the money to himself without detection.

In August 1909, Jahns went to Spokane to hire a housekeeper. There he met Agnes Jansen, a widow who had immigrated to the United States a few months before. Jahns seemed like an upstanding citizen, so Jansen accepted his offer of work. She had been working at the Jahns farm for three months when Jahns went on another trip to Spokane. He stopped at the house of Margaret Aherns, where Jansen had been living before she went to Cedonia. Mrs. Aherns gave him a letter that had arrived for Jansen. He promised to pass it on. They had grown quite fond of each other, he told Mrs. Aherns, and they intended to get married.

However, his next action seems to contradict his supposed good intentions. While in Spokane, he asked a German mail clerk to translate the contents of the letter. Though he claimed to be able to speak German, he said he could not read it. He was greatly pleased with what he learned. It seemed that Jansen was about to receive a considerable amount of money. About $3,500 in American money had been deposited in a Berlin bank for her and would soon be forwarded to her in America.

The news apparently changed Jahns's romantic ideas to thoughts of murder. He decided to kill Jansen for her money. She suspected nothing when the two rode out in the wagon on the night of October 27. Just a few hours later, she was dead from two gunshots to the head. The bonfire left little evidence of her existence. But there was enough.

Jahns thought he had come up with a foolproof plan, but it started to unravel right away. Unbeknownst to Jahns, a man named Al Stayt had seen him pull up to the Hergesheimer ranch about three o'clock in the morning. He recognized Jahns, though he couldn't see who was with him. Then a man named Swede Johnson came up, noticing the fire in which Jahns burned Jansen's body. Jahns casually talked to him about a mule trade, telling Johnson about how one of his animals had become ill, so he had to send Jansen on to Blue Creek with a passing stranger. He hoped that Johnson wouldn't realize what was going on just a few feet away.

About six in the morning, M. D. Taylor, who owned property nearby, noticed the fire and went to investigate. Taylor saw the huge pile of burning logs, a pyre about six feet high and six feet wide. Some of the logs were so large, he knew they had to have been hauled into place by a horse. Taylor figured the fire had been burning for several hours. Jahns lay sound asleep in his wagon nearby, but Taylor woke him up and asked what he was doing there. Again Jahns told his story of taking his housekeeper to the railway station at Blue Creek when one of the horses became sick. He met someone going the same way and sent her on with him so she didn't miss her train. The story satisfied Taylor for the moment.

When the fire was nearly burned out and was in no danger of spreading, Jahns left the scene. He continued down the road to Summit Valley, eight miles west of Blue Creek. He met F. F. Dorm and J. W. Morrison on the way, and Jahns told them he was going to Chewelah to catch a train. They drove with each other for a while before splitting up. After spending the night at the Cline residence in Summit Valley, Jahns hired one of the Cline sons to drive him to Blue Creek, where he checked his luggage to Spokane. He paid Mr. Cline to drive his rig back to Cedonia, then he rode the train as far as Hillyard, just outside Spokane. From there he bought a ticket to Davenport, thirty miles west. He walked into the Bank of Davenport to withdraw money from Jansen's account, pretending to be her husband and saying that he had her power of attorney. He showed the cashier, M. W. Anderson, the deed to his property as collateral. He was still using the name Logan at the time. When Anderson called the bank's branch in Hunters, he learned that this James Logan was wanted for a serious crime. He did not give Jahns the money he requested, so Jahns left in a huff and checked into a nearby hotel.

Meanwhile, curiosity got the better of Elmer and Ira Gifford and their uncle Charles Gifford, who had seen Jahns's bonfire while hunting. They returned to the site of the fire. Jahns was gone by then, but he left some terrible evidence behind. As they picked through the ashes of the fire, Elmer Gifford found the remains of a human hand. As soon as the Giffords saw the gruesome remnant, they rode to the nearest farm and called Sheriff W. H. Graham at Colville. A few hours later, Sheriff Graham arrived with the coroner and the prosecutor. After inspecting the area, Graham found a box of .32 shells, a hat-pin, wires from a woman's hat, belt buckles, corset stays, and a piece of dental bridgework. He also noticed wagon tracks leading away from the scene and a bloodstain by the gate. Rain earlier in the day had created muddy tracks that were easy to follow. The lawman followed the tracks back to Jahns's farm.

Jahns had not arrived back at home yet, but while the sheriff talked with hired hands Tisth and Hilton, Johnny Cline drove up with Jahns's wagon. Cline told Graham that he had driven Jahns's team back from Blue Creek while Jahns went on to Spokane. From there, he reported, Jahns was going to visit Davenport before coming back to Cedonia.

Instinct and experience told Sheriff Graham that Jahns had killed a woman and then burned her to get rid of the evidence. He didn't yet know who the woman was, but he figured that she must have had something the murderer wanted. He called Sheriff Gardner in Davenport and asked him to keep his eyes open for the suspect.

Gardner didn't take long to track down Jahns. His officers found him drinking in a Davenport saloon, probably still trying to decide how to get Jansen's money. Gardner's men approached him and asked him his name. When he said it was James Logan, they told him he was under arrest. When he asked why, they told him he was wanted for the murder of a woman in Stevens County. At first he seemed surprised, but then he sighed and walked away with them. Gardner led him to the local jail while other officers seized Jahns's possessions from his hotel.

Jahns possessed a cornucopia of incriminating evidence. There was a deed to the Baslington ranch in Cedonia, transferring it from a George Hilton to James Logan, notarized by E. B. Bernhardt of Republic, Washington. There was a notary seal, made not by Talcott Bros. Jewelers in Olympia, like most notary seals were, but by Spokane Stamp Works. There were two rubber stamps used to stamp the name of a payee on a check. He had a stamp used by railroad employees to date tickets and a canceling perforator. There was an advertising flyer for inks and a box that contained papers from a safety deposit box in Chicago. He held checks written by D. R. Shively a few days before he disappeared and a letter from James Heatherington addressed to Shively dated February 24, 1908. Jahns's valise contained a letter addressed to Agnes Janson in care of Mrs. Margaret Ahrens in Spokane.

The unfolding details of the case were getting interesting for Sheriff Graham. He suspected that he might clear up more than one case with this arrest. Deputy Frank Coontz of Daisy picked up Hilton and brought him to the Colville jail for questioning. Hilton admitted that he was Jahns's nephew. He said he came to Stevens County from Nebraska in the spring of 1908 after not seeing his uncle for twenty years. He acted surprised when the sheriff showed him the deed transferring Hilton's property to James Logan. He said he had not sold any of his land to Uncle Frank.

Frank? So James Logan wasn't his real name. He sent pictures of both Jahns and Hilton to police departments around the northwest to see if anyone recognized them. The pictures reached Sheriff DeHaven in Bellingham, who recognized both pictures. He told Graham that he knew the older man as Frank Romandorf and the younger man as his son Ed. Graham asked DeHaven to come to Davenport to identify the suspect.

Sheriff DeHaven and a Sheriff Williams positively identified Jahns as the man they knew as Frank Romandorf. DeHaven had once questioned him about some stolen cattle. Williams accused him of murdering the real James Logan and assuming his identity. Jahns denied it, but then stupidly he remarked, "I suppose when you start trailing me back and find out I was once in South Africa, you will accuse me of doing things like that down there, too." Unfortunately for Jahns, this statement merely heightened the suspicion surrounding him.

So Graham started asking around. Jahns's neighbors in Cedonia told Graham about how Jahns had bragged about the great fortune he made in South Africa but lost in Nebraska. On a whim, Graham sent Jahns's photos to the South African police, who replied that the picture was of William Frederick Jahns, a man suspected of killing eight men in diamond heists. They had traced him as far as New Orleans before losing his trail. Now Graham finally knew the real name of his suspect.

While the state was building its case against Jahns, hundreds of curiosity seekers visited the jail, hoping to catch a glimpse of the murderer. At the time, he was being held only for the murder of Agnes Janson. Janson Jahns mostly kept to himself and huddled in a corner to avoid being gawked at. When the official court photographer came to take his picture, a hundred men gathered around to see what the criminal looked like. What they saw did not seem to be very threatening.

Jahns was about fifty-five years old, with a sallow complexion, thin face, and broad features. He had gray eyes, gray hair and mustache, and weighed about 130 pounds. He still spoke with a strong German accent.

Graham tracked down Jahns's family in Seattle. His wife, Margaret, and daughter, Bessie, both lived there. Margaret admitted to being married to a man named Frank Romandorf and that the man known as George Hilton was their son Ed Romandorf. She said they had been married in Pennsylvania, then moved to Nebraska and on to Washington. Evidently, she did not know her husband's real name or that he had been arrested. The last time she had seen Jahns was in August, when she and her daughter visited his Stevens County ranch.

Jahns's trial for the murder of Agnes Jansen began on January 4, 1910. The case caused quite a sensation. Every hotel room in Colville was booked with those who were attending the trial. The courtroom was packed every day, and a large number of the spectators were women. Judge Carey had to warn them frequently about keeping the "screaming babies" from making noise or they would have to leave. He also told them to remove their hats so that everyone could see. High school kids skipped school to attend the trial. Judge Carey warned them about giggling in the courtroom. Later he instructed his bailiffs to prevent any school-age children from entering the courtroom at all. Everyone was eager to get a glimpse of the infamous murderer.

A man named Kirkpatrick tried the case for the state. It took several days and 150 candidates before an impartial jury was finally selected. Because some people believed that Agnes Jansen was still alive somewhere, the prosecution first showed evidence that proved she was dead. Human bones, a brooch, a gold crucifix, and some corset stays found in the fire were introduced to show that a human being had been burned in the fire and that the evidence clearly proved it was Jansen. Graham testified to finding the bullets that were the same caliber as a revolver found in Jahns's possession. The Giffords also told about the items they had found in the fire.

Others testified to Jahns's actions during the time immediately before and after the murder. Tisth verified that Jansen was indeed living at the ranch as a housekeeper and was still there on the night of October 27. George Hilton, also known as Ed Romandorf, admitted that he helped Jahns get the wagon ready for the trip to Blue Creek. He noted that Jahns and Jansen left about midnight that night. At the time, he noticed that the wagon turned the opposite direction from that normally taken to reach Blue Creek. Swede Johnson testified to seeing Jahns at the Hergesheimer farm during the early morning hours, and M. D. Taylor said he had seen him there around seven o'clock in the morning. Al Stayt testified that he had seen Jahns both on the road in the early hours of the morning and later at the Cline place.

Coroner Cook testified to finding human remains on the Hergesheimer property. He identified human vertebrae and teeth. Several other experts were brought in to identify the bones and teeth as belonging to a human and not an animal.

Several of Jansen's friends testified regarding the jewelry that they knew she wore. Mrs. Ahrens recalled the dental work that Jansen had and mentioned that Jahns had visited her and taken Jansen's mail. J. K. Lehman related how he had translated the letter for a man named Logan.

With the overwhelming evidence that provided method, motive, and opportunity for Jahns to kill Agnes Jansen, his various land schemes hardly needed mentioning. All the various seals and stamps and inks used to produce fake documents found in his possession were not brought out at trial. The one exception was the notarized deed, transferring the Baslington ranch from Hilton to James Logan. Mr. Howell from Olympia came to identify the notary seal used on the deed. He stated that his office was responsible for certifying all notaries and that there was no one named E. B. Bernhardt certified in Washington. The defense objected to this testimony, saying it was irrelevant. But the prosecution argued it was necessary to show the extreme measures Jahns took to acquire something that didn't belong to him.

By the time the defense took the stand, the outcome of the trial looked bleak for Jahns. At first his lawyers had decided against an insanity defense. They believed that Jahns was completely sane and evil. But as they neared the end of the trial, they changed their minds after talking with their client. The day before the defense was to present its case, Jahns spilled the beans. He claimed that people were constantly following him and waiting for their chance to kill him. He only killed them first to protect himself. He said he had run away from Germany to avoid being conscripted into the German army. He ran to South Africa, where he killed eight men and stole $85,000 worth of diamonds. He later lost the money in a business deal in Nebraska. He admitted to using the name Frank Romandorf most of the time he was in America.

He went on to tell about the people he had killed since coming to America. He admitted to killing Agnes Janson and burning her in the fire. He also told them he had killed James Logan and disposed of his body in a culvert near his house. He admitted killing D. R. Shively by poisoning his drink and murdering Fred Helms and Jack Green in Maple Falls. They each had property that he wanted, he said. He stated that he had killed many other people in many other countries from Canada to Africa.

The defense figured their case was hopeless, but they did what they could. Most of the witnesses they called were questioned about Jahns's state of mind in an attempt to show that Jahns was unstable. They wanted to establish that Jahns was "non compos mentis," meaning he was not responsible for his actions. The most convincing evidence to this fact was the way Jahns acted in the courtroom. Sometimes he would babble incoherently; other times he would shout out loud.

The state recalled three witnesses to say that they had never seen any strange behavior from Jahns. I. A. Keith, who lived in Addy and had known Jahns since he lived in Nebraska, said he had never known Jahns to exhibit unusual behavior. Sheriff Graham and Jailer Lynch agreed with Keith's assessment.

After only an hour of deliberation, the jury pronounced Jahns guilty. In that hour, the jury members had voted twice. The first vote was ten to two for conviction. The second vote was unanimous. Jahns did not seem particularly surprised or upset about the verdict. When he was returned to his jail cell, other inmates asked him how the trial had gone. He told them he had been found guilty. He was taken to the Walla Walla State Penitentiary and hanged as scheduled on April 21, 1911.

Rustlers!

Although Washington is not often thought of as a "wild, wild West" state, it has had its share of trouble with stereotyped Wild West characters like rustlers. Both cattle and horses were prime targets of thieves in the nineteenth and early twentieth centuries. The next town could be miles away in the wide-open spaces of eastern Washington. Until the 1920s, horses were the most common mode of transportation for the state's citizens. In fact, horses were the most valuable piece of property a man could own, next to his house. If a man owned cattle he was considered wealthy. A man's steer meant food on the table or money in his pocket. So when horses or cattle were stolen, either a few at a time or a whole herd, the victims took it very seriously.

Several gangs of horse thieves operated throughout the Columbia Basin, a perfect location for men who stole horses for a living. Crisscrossed with canyons and coulees, the basin provided perfect places to hide horses out of sight of the law. Much of the terrain looked the same, a factor that confused pursuers and protected rustlers. Though the region was arid, there was plenty of grass for stolen livestock to eat. The region was sparsely settled, so there were few witnesses to a man's thievery and even fewer who would hunt him down. Many ranchers didn't even bother corralling their horses, so they were prime targets of horse thieves.

Thieves commonly used Moses Coulee in central Washington to hide their stolen animals. This canyonlike formation was far from a population center, and there was usually water and grass for the horses in its bottom. It was often cooler in the summer, too. When the stolen horses were rested, the thieves drove them north to British Columbia to sell them. More often than not, the same thieves would steal horses in Canada and drive them back to the United States. They sold the Canadian horses in eastern or southern Washington. The thieves were careful to avoid being seen in the same place twice in a row.

One of the largest gangs of cattle rustlers operated out of Dayton, in Columbia County, in the early 1890s. George Young was the ringleader of the gang. He set up a slaughterhouse on Patit Creek just north of Dayton, and his operatives rustled cattle in Columbia, Garfield, and Asotin Counties. The thieves brought the stolen cattle to his slaughterhouse, where Young butchered them. Once the steers were cut into steaks, no one could tell whose brand was originally on the hide. Young then sold the meat at his retail store. Young was eventually captured and served time in prison, but he would give no information about his cohorts. The rest of his gang was eventually rounded up, but the law had quite a time bringing them in.

The main suspects were Billy Lloyd, Bud Pettijohn, Chan Taylor, and John Long. Columbia County Sheriff A. H. Weatherford and Deputy Albert Allen solved the case. In the summer of 1894, the suspects stole some cattle from John Powell in Asotin County. They already had a buyer named John Church in Columbia County. When the rustlers arrived with the herd, Church asked the men to drive the steers to the Fred Gritman ranch on the Tucannon River. He joined them for the drive, not knowing that the cattle were stolen. But somewhere along the line he became suspicious and snuck a message off to the sheriff.

Deputy Allen led a posse consisting of the Garfield County sheriff, two deputies, and four citizens to Alpowa Creek, thinking the rustlers would pass by. On August 4, Lloyd and Pettijohn rode up, and Allen told them to give themselves up. Lloyd pulled his gun, jumped off his horse, and started firing. Allen and the others returned the fire. Lloyd and Pettijohn both fled on foot, firing at the lawmen over their shoulders. The posse chased them for about two hundred yards until both men surrendered. Lloyd was wounded slightly in two places on his left leg. Pettijohn had two wounds in his left thigh. None of the officers were injured.

Some men kept the rustlers in custody while the others looked for Taylor and Long. They soon caught up with Taylor, who was driving about sixty head of cattle down a canyon. He gave up without a fight. Long was never found.

The three men were taken to the Garfield County seat in Pomeroy. Lloyd was convicted in April 1895 and sentenced to three years in prison. Taylor received a similar sentence. For some reason, Pettijohn was acquitted, even though it was obvious he had been involved. Perhaps the jury felt he had already been punished by the gunshot wound that crippled him.

At the northern edge of the state, a den of horse thieves operated out of Ferry County, which consisted mostly of large stands of timber, with the town of Republic right in the middle. A late-blooming boomtown, trading in miners' gold, Republic attracted its share of riffraff. By 1899, the county was plagued by horse and cattle thieves. The Ferry County gang had an interesting technique. They would steal the cattle or horses and hide them out of the county. Then, when a reward was offered, they would show up with the cattle or horses and collect the reward.

The problems with the gang ended when Deputy Sheriff Griswold shot and killed the ringleader, Charles McDonald, and arrested his partner, Frank Draper.

Another gang operated out of Grant County. This group stole horses from isolated ranches and homesteads in the Spokane area. Then they drove the horses to the scablands and coulees of northern Grant County. There was so much broken rock and gravel that the thieves could travel through the area without leaving tracks.

The thieves hid the horses on Steamboat Rock in the Grand Coulee. Made out of tough volcanic basalt, Steamboat Rock was more like a mesa than it was a rock. A narrow trail snaked up the side of the rock, and the rustlers drove the horses up to the top. Then they blocked the entrance to the trail to camouflage it. A depression in the top of the rock held water most of the year, so the horses could water there and munch on some good grass until the thieves took them into town for sale. Later the thieves took the horses to the Yakima Valley as if they were ordinary ranchers with horses for sale.

Often, at the same time some thieves were in Yakima selling horses, their partners would be in Yakima stealing horses. The rustlers would ride away with the horses and take them to Steamboat Rock for hiding. They would lay low for a while, then take those horses to sell in the Spokane/Coeur d'Alene, Idaho area. In this way, the thieves created their own markets for horses! In some cases, buyers unsuspectingly bought their own horses back.

By the turn of the century, citizens started fighting back against rustlers. But the outlaws weren't done yet. Through the first few years of the twentieth century, a rash of thefts occurred throughout the Horse Heaven Hills country of southern Washington and the Yakima Valley, where the country was hilly and easy to hide in.

In May of 1906, the law caught up with a Yakima County outlaw gang when Walla Walla County Deputy Byrnes captured a man calling himself Bill Thorpe. Thorpe was actually Dick Dymond, part of the Dymond brothers gang. Two months later, the law captured another member of the Dymond gang, John McKerrall. There was a brief gunfight, during which McKerrall was wounded. Two weeks earlier, McKerrall had stolen two valuable horses from Howard S. Amon of Richland, his former employer. Sheriff Alex McNeill of Prosser recovered Amon's horses from Fort Simcoe, along with four Indian ponies that had been stolen in Zillah.

The Dymonds were getting nervous, but they continued their thievery. The end nearly came one day when Deputy Sheriff J. M. Edwards passed them on his way to Goldendale. He had never seen them, so at first he didn't realize who they were. The gang quickly took this small advantage to make their getaway.

Toward the end of July, Sheriff McNeill and Deputy Byrnes finally captured George Dymond at Wallula. He was armed with a Colt revolver when they found him, but he did not resist arrest.

Another gang was broken up in March of 1908. This gang operated in the Horse Heaven Hills country, south of the Columbia River. They shipped their captured horses out of Wallula to places as far away as Miles City, Montana, and St. Louis, Missouri. They were crafty men and evaded the law for quite some time. The thieves housed their booty in barns and corrals. When questioned, the rustlers claimed they were caring for the animals for someone else. The law could not prove that they were holding stolen property.

But the law finally got a break and captured the leaders of the gang, John Tycke and his two sons, John Jr. and Richard, in Wallula. Paul Kruger and J. A. McIntyre were also wanted as part of the gang. Deputy Sheriff Charles Painter of Walla Walla chased Kruger all the way to Burns, Oregon, before he caught up with him. Sheriff A. K. Richardson of Harney County, Oregon, captured McIntyre even farther south and brought him back to Washington.

A month later, George Beard was captured at Lind, in Adams County. He was wanted on an outstanding warrant from 1903. He had been arrested for horse theft then, but he had skipped town when he was released on bail. Painter hurried to Lind to bring Beard back to Walla Walla for a long-deserved trial.

About the same time, Deputy Sheriff Cummins of Wallula arrested Rolla Warner at Hover, on the Benton County side of the Columbia River. Four other men who had four stolen horses in their possession were arrested at the same time. Their apprehension is thought to be the last arrest of horse thieves patrolling the Horse Heaven Hills area. Cummins turned Warner over to Sheriff Til Taylor of Pendleton, Oregon, who held an outstanding warrant on him.

The remaining horse thieves had one last hurrah in July of 1909. The Press Connors gang worked from Franklin County all the way to the Canadian border. Several county sheriffs held a conference at the office of Sheriff A. J. Cross of Ritzville, the county seat of Adams County, to discuss what to do about the horse thieves. They had a list of nineteen prominent farmers rumored to belong to the gang, so they started rounding them up. The first six to be brought in were John Baize, Carl Blankenship, "Montana Kid" Gregg, a man named Dawley, Ralph Carter, and Press Connors. Waldo Dent of Pasco and John Peters, Ral Estep, George Weeks, and E. J. Edwards of Othello were also arrested because of information provided to the sheriff by John Baize. They arrested Ralph Carter of Colfax for stealing a horse from a well-known Franklin County rancher as well as many other victims. All nineteen men were eventually arrested.

Baize and Carter were sentenced to one to five years at the state reformatory in Monroe. Blankenship, a former college student at Pullman, received a ten-year suspended sentence.

After that, horse and cattle thefts in Washington were reduced to very small-scale operations, and the perpetrators were usually captured. By that time, cars and trains replaced horses as the primary mode of travel, so horse theft died out as a favorite crime of outlaws. Cattle were still in high demand as a food animal, but the law could get after the thieves quickly in an automobile. The crime of rustling came to an end.

Max Levy

The 1890s were a wild time for Port Townsend, Washington. The town was the port of entry for goods and immigrants coming into the United States from Canada. It was a busy port that shipped timber and the local fish harvest far and wide. After a long day's work, sailors trudged into the nearest saloon to whet their whistles. Trouble was brewing between the union and non-union sailors, and they kept a wary eye on each other as they drank. On August 11, 1893, the uneasy truce came to an end.

About 8.00 p.m., someone assaulted a non-union sailor. A few minutes later he escaped, but he was in bad condition when he reached the Latona Saloon. The Latona, owned by Max Levy, was the headquarters of the non-union sailors. Whether the sailor's non-union status was the cause of the beating is not known. But it would soon become an excuse for an all-out brawl.

Some union sailors followed the man to the Latona. Someone sent word to the union headquarters, and a large union force converged on the saloon. At first the two groups just taunted each other from either side of the street. Then one of the union men tried to enter the Latona for a drink. Levy stopped him at the door. Two of his employees, Charles Gunderson and barkeeper Robert Kirk, picked up their weapons and prepared to do battle. The three men warned the union man that he better stay away or there would be trouble.

The union men ignored the warning and swarmed the saloon. No one knows who fired the first shot or threw the first punch. Union sailor James Connor was shot twice, in the right shoulder and in the right hip. Otto Anderson, a waiter who had nothing to do with the dispute, was slightly wounded in the stomach from a stray bullet. Ricardo Gueraro was hit in the right leg. He was not part of the dispute, but had just come into town and had been drawn to the altercation by the noise. Union sailor Joseph Dixon attempted to smash the window of the Latona but badly cut his arm on the glass. Someone also tried to hit Levy's wife, who was watching from the second-story window, with a rock. Fortunately, he missed his target.

The fight went on for some time before the police could get it under control. Officer Brophy escorted Levy, Gunderson, and Kirk to the jail to protect them from the mob. The crowd was in an ugly mood and wanted to lynch the men. As it was, every ground-floor window of the Latona Saloon was broken. The inside looked like a hurricane hit it.

Early the next morning, the saloon district showed signs of resuming the argument of the previous night. About 10:00 a.m., an argument broke out between the union and non-union sailors. But this time, officers were ready. They broke it up before it got too far. One shot was fired, but no one was hurt. Several others were arrested and charged with inciting a riot and for property damage to the Latona Saloon. They were held in a different part of the jail from where Levy and Gunderson were staying.

By that time, Levy was known as the king of the shanghai-ers. The practice of shanghaiing, forcing a man to sail on a ship against his will, had been around for hundreds of years. But it wasn't until the 1850s that it became known as shanghaiing at San Francisco's Barbary Coast. Being "sent to Shanghai" was what happened when a man was knocked out and placed on a ship on its way to the Orient. The men who engaged in this practice became known as "crimpers."

Levy was born in San Francisco so he was well familiar with the practice. He prospected for a short time in the Klondike before coming to Port Townsend in 1889. He became part owner of the Chicago Clothing Company with a man named Thomas Newman. A short time later he married Lucy Hogg, daughter of a local sea captain. They would have one son, named James Maxwell Levy.

Soon after his arrival in Port Townsend, Levy met a man named Ed Sims. Sims was a respectable businessman and in fact was a deputy U.S. shipping commissioner. His position suited Levy just fine. Since 1895, a man was required to sign on a ship before the consul of the country that owned the ship or before a U.S. shipping commissioner. The sailor was supposed to be fully aware of what he was doing (i.e., not intoxicated) before he would be accepted or he would be denied passage. With Sims as commissioner, it was easy for Levy to get away with certain business arrangements.

Sims's financial backing also allowed Levy to purchase a share in a sailors' boardinghouse and saloon. The boarding-house was located on the waterfront, just across the street from the City Hall. The rear of the building opened on the dock. It was a handsome brick structure that got the attention of sailors just coming into port. Many chose it as a place to stay. But many sailors did not have the money to pay for the lodging, so Levy would lend them enough to pay for their room and board.

When a ship came into port, it often needed extra hands. The captain would call upon Levy to supply some men. For each man supplied, Levy received some money from the ship's captain. This included a "finder's fee" for Levy and an advance on the sailor's wages, which paid off the money the sailor owed to Levy for staying at his boardinghouse. This arrangement made the sailor indebted to the ship's owner and earned a fat profit for Levy.

The problem was, some sailors weren't amenable to going out to sea at that particular time. Maybe they were waiting for a particular ship to come in. Maybe they were too sick to go to sea. Some of the men the boardinghouse owners signed up weren't even sailors. But it didn't matter. Levy wasn't too picky when it came to giving the ship's captains what they wanted.

Levy wasn't one to get his hands dirty either. He just gave the orders to his "runners" and then stood back to collect the money. These runners didn't hesitate to use force whenever necessary to get their quota of sailors. They waited until a man passed out when he had too much to drink. Sometimes they didn't have time to wait, so they put "knock-out drops" in a man's drink. Once the man was out cold, they would dump him in a skiff and row him out to the waiting ship. Sometimes they used the town's soiled doves to help them separate the sailor from his valuables before they left him onboard. By the time the man woke up the next day, he was far out to sea.

Levy chose his victims carefully. He never shanghaied an Indian. By that time, most Indians were under the jurisdiction of the U.S. Bureau of Indian Affairs. So if there was a complaint, the federal government would soon come poking around. Levy wanted no part of that. He also avoided taking local residents. If his runners couldn't find any professional sailors, they took farmhands or loggers or soldiers or even vagrants. For the most part, a man's race didn't matter one iota.

Levy's most notorious runner was a man named Gunderson. He used any method to do Levy's bidding, including beating people into insensibility. One time, Gunderson and fellow runner Chilean Pete snuck aboard a British ship to convince the sailors to desert. The runners would pay them to desert, but they would get double their money back when the ship's captains went to Levy to hire another crew. Unfortunately, this particular time they were caught in the act. They quickly jumped off the ship and frantically rowed toward Levy's boardinghouse.

The ship's mate and boatswain gave chase in a small rowboat. When they caught up with the shanghaiers, Gunderson tried to knock them out with an oar. The ship's mate fired his gun, fatally wounding Chilean Pete and wounding Gunderson in the shoulder. A trial followed the shooting, but the jury found the mate not guilty since Chilean Pete had been engaged in piracy. Gunderson was charged, too, but escaped conviction by claiming he had not boarded the ship and that he was there at the invitation of the sailors.

Levy's favorite tactic was to dispose of one crew so that he could be paid to supply another. He lured them with promises of better conditions that he knew about on another ship. Of course the conditions really were no better and were sometimes worse. But the sailors didn't know any better when they did what he wanted. On one occasion, he succeeded in convincing three different crews to abandon the ship America before the ship was finally able to sail with a full crew.

One man who had been shanghaied on a ship to Hong Kong swore he would get even. It took two years before he finally got back to Port Townsend, and he headed straight for

Levy's office. When he found him, two of his runners were talking to him. Though outnumbered, he jumped on them anyway. It wasn't long before he lay unconscious on the ground.

Eventually Gunderson shanghaied one victim too many. He was trying to get a man drunk, but it was taking too long. So he finally knocked him down with a bar stool and then kicked him in the face. The man fought back, but Gunderson was just too powerful. He dragged him aboard a ship bound for Australia. As soon as he could, the sailor came back to Port Townsend. He went straight to Levy's boardinghouse. There he accosted Gunderson and stabbed him seven times. Gunderson survived, but tendons in his neck and arms were severely damaged. He ended his relationship with Levy and lived out the rest of his days as a fisherman.

When he was arrested for the altercation at his saloon in 1893, Levy went to trial for assault. Levy was defended by A.R. Coleman, from the shipowner's association of San Francisco. Coleman explained how Gunderson had only fired warning shots into the floor. But when the union men ignored it and lunged toward them, Levy and Gunderson were just defending themselves. Two non-union sailors named Ralston and Lanstrum testified that Levy had not been armed and that he had only come out from behind the bar to try to settle things down.

Of course the union men had a different story. Their attorneys, James Hamilton Lewis and E. S. Lyons, claimed Levy had kicked and beat up the victim without provocation. Union agents McGlynn and Benedikton also claimed that the fight had not been a union vs. non-union issue. They said a man had gone into the saloon because he had lost a ring there two weeks ago. He had simply gone in to demand the return of his ring. The fight started when he was kicked out of the saloon.

The first trial ended with a hung jury. The second jury acquitted Levy, even though there had been witnesses to the event. The others charged with inciting a riot were also acquitted. Shortly afterward, some of the union issues were settled. The union agreed to a $5-per-month salary reduction on deep-sea vessels. Other salary reductions were made.

Levy went right back to his old tricks, shanghaiing sailors and relieving them of their money. Levy and his runners once beat up a ship captain and one of his sailors because they dared to hire a sailor without Levy's consent. He still engaged in his favorite trick, which was to run off a crew so that a ship's captain would have to pay him to assemble a new one.

Levy also cut corners whenever he could. He generally received about $90 a man and about $20 to pay for clothes and other things the sailor would need while he was at sea. One time, Levy supplied about twenty sailors for a British ship. But before the ship could sail, the sailors threatened to mutiny. The ship's captain called Levy about the problem. Levy called the British consul to help. For once, Levy's plan backfired.

After talking to each sailor, the consul discovered that the clothing supplied was woefully inadequate. In fact, some of it looked like it could have been taken out of trash dumpsters or off corpses. Some of it was even women's clothing! The consul discovered what Levy had done and told him he would have to supply appropriate clothing. Levy grudgingly did what he had to, but it was one of the few times he didn't get away with it.

Early in 1896, Levy was again in trouble with the law. He shanghaied two men for a British ship that was in port. He and one of his runners, Thomas Newman, rowed them out to the ship and left them there. As he was rowing away, one of the shanghaied men jumped overboard, trying to escape. Thomas Breen saw him jump and went to rescue him. Levy beat up the man for his trouble. Levy was charged with assault with a deadly weapon, but the case was dismissed.

In May 1896, Levy and Newman were charged with stealing some baggage belonging to a sailor named Alex Von Hagen. The charge was brought before Commissioner James G. Swan. Newman had stored Von Hagen's baggage onboard his ship. Then he asked Von Hagen to sign a promissory note for $50 that he supposedly owed Levy for his room and board. Von Hagen refused because he thought the bill was much too high. Newman refused to give Von Hagen his luggage until he paid.

Levy told a slightly different story. He admitted that they took the luggage. He said that he would have gladly given it to anybody who had come after it; all they had to do was ask. Swan dismissed the case after ordering an assistant to escort Levy and Von Hagen to get the missing baggage.

The incident must have left Levy in a foul mood. Just a few days later, he was involved in an altercation that would land him back in jail. A sailor named Charles M. Carlson was leaning on a railing outside the Red Front Clothing House when Levy approached him. He threw a rock at Carlson and injured his eye.

Levy was charged with assault and battery. Ex-judge Morris B. Sachs defended Levy. Originally the case was slated to be heard by City Magistrate Jones, but Sachs asked for a change of venue to Judge Woods's court. Rather than place his case in the hands of one man, the prosecuting attorney moved for a jury trial. It took some time before the case was placed on the docket. Finally Carlson got his day in court.

Carlson testified that the assault was totally uncalled for and unprovoked. Three other men, William Debbert, Eugene Thurlow, and Charles Webber, were in the street nearby, and all saw Levy hit Carlson. They could not say what provoked the assault or if it was justified, but could verify that Levy did strike Carlson. None of them saw Carlson strike back.

Levy testified in his own defense. He said that Carlson was interfering with his boardinghouse business. He said Carlson was trying to entice men away. The night he hit him, he saw Carlson standing in front of the Red Front store and decided to talk to him about what he was doing. While talking, he said Carlson kicked him in the stomach. He was only defending himself when he hit Carlson back.

Two other witnesses said they saw Carlson strike first. Webber and Debbert said they did not see Carlson kick Levy. Carlson also denied that he had struck Levy. Due to the conflicting testimony, the jury could not reach a decision. Contemporary papers suggested that many people sympathized with the crimpers.

In 1906, shanghaiing was brought to an abrupt halt. New laws prohibited any runner, shipping concern, or steamship agency from hiring a sailor who was drunk. The law also stated that once a sailor was onboard, he could leave for just cause by bringing it before the board of commissioners. Steep fines were imposed against those who failed to obey the law, anywhere from $200 to $500 for each occurrence.

This law made it difficult for Levy to continue on as he had before. He kept his hand in the business for a little while though, taking care to keep a very low profile. His business was damaged further when steamships started rapidly replacing sailing vessels. Fewer hands were needed to man the new ships, which further eroded his boardinghouse business. Unions were also doing a better job of protecting sailors' rights. By 1910, Levy gave it up. In 1912 he moved his family to San Francisco. He died there in 1931.

His financial partner, Sims, remained in Port Townsend. He earned a handsome profit from the two canneries he owned in Blaine and Port Townsend. He also dabbled in mining, logging, and oil, and eventually became a state legislator. He died in September 1945.

Roy Olmstead

Disgusted with working conditions in Washington's harbors, Roy Olmstead quit his job as a Seattle shipyard laborer and joined the Seattle Police Department in 1906. He quickly built a reputation for being smart and competent. In 1910 he was promoted to sergeant. He became a lieutenant in 1917, the youngest man to attain the rank. He knew Mayor Gill personally, and he commanded such respect that his advice was often sought when deciding punishment for convicted criminals. Before long he began accepting bribes to give certain recommendations to the judge.

During Olmstead's stint on the force, he noted certain trends in crime. Since the time he had become a lieutenant, the sale, manufacture, or import of liquor had become illegal. He watched with interest as two rival gangs competed for the monopoly on the illegal rum trade. Jack Marquett led one of the gangs. Olmstead knew him because Marquett had once been a police officer. Logan and Fred Billingsley led the other gang. Eventually the two gangs engaged in a huge gun battle that resulted in several deaths and left many wounded. The rum trade was in disarray. Olmstead saw his opportunity to step into the gap.

He first appeared on the wrong side of the law early on the morning of March 22, 1920. On that day, a tugboat approached the shore of Brown's Bay, near Meadowdale in Snohomish County. Just when the boat reached the shore, lights came on and voices called out. Somehow Prohibition agents had found out about the delivery. The men who were picking up

147

the liquor scattered and ran. Agents fired after them. One was grazed, but they all got away, including Roy Olmstead, who escaped in his car. Unfortunately for him, one of the agents spotted him and recognized him.

Later that afternoon, Olmstead was not surprised when police officers knocked at his door. They took him in for bootlegging. He was fined $500 and dismissed from the police force. Olmstead cheerfully paid the fine and left the courtroom. There was much more money where that came from.

Olmstead immediately began building the largest bootlegging operation in the state. He found eleven other men who each donated $1,000 to set up the business. He hired sailors, dispatchers, bookkeepers, salesmen, and many others. Some of the men on his payroll were police officers. He used his connections from the police force to get people to look the other way in regard to his illegal activities. He studied the markets and the liquor suppliers.

He usually bought his liquor in British Columbia, but there was an export duty of $20 on every case bound for the United States, so Olmstead cleared his ships for Mexico, where there was no duty. That savings helped him keep the prices down for his customers while still creating a tidy profit for himself.

He soon owned a fleet of boats that cruised the Puget Sound powered by surplus World War I Liberty airplane engines. He shipped two thousand to four thousand cases each trip.

Olmstead's rumrunners took the liquor to D'Arcy Island in the Haro Strait between Vancouver Island and San Juan Island. Not only was the small island remote, it was also dangerous. Hidden reefs around the island made its waters difficult to navigate. The local weather was unpredictable, keeping the Coast

Guard and Prohibition agents away. In addition, a leper colony on the island kept curiosity seekers away. The colony's keeper kept an eye on Olmstead's liquor until he could pick it up. The rumrunners would eventually load the booze on small boats and take it to Puget Sound. From there it would be taken to warehouses and garages to be divided into small lots. It would be divided into still smaller lots at saloons and restaurants and private stocks.

This arrangement and Olmstead's quantity discount allowed him to undercut his competition by as much as 30 percent. Soon he was selling two hundred cases of liquor a day and grossing more than $200,000 a month. The competition forced many smaller operators out of business. Some became pirates, lurking beyond the shadows on D'Arcy Island ready to rob the booze-laden boats. Others decided the best way to stay in business was to go work for Olmstead. His success allowed him to buy a large ocean freighter and a farm where he could hide liquor. He kept an office in Seattle's Henry Building, from which he distributed thousands of cases of whiskey and other liquor.

Olmstead always seemed to stay just one step ahead of the law. He used what he knew about how it operated to his advantage. For example, knowing that wiretapping was illegal in the state, he frequently used the telephone to conduct trans-actions. Realistically, though, he knew the police were listening in. So he set up deliveries of contraband liquor over the phone, describing exactly where and when the delivery would take place. Later he called back the customer on a pay phone and set up a new time and place. The police would dutifully show up at a dark beach while the delivery successfully took place somewhere else.

One of Olmstead's most reliable employees was a man named Prosper Graignic. He had a forty-five-foot-long, gas-powered boat, with two three-hundred-horsepower engines. Graignic's instincts were uncanny when it came to navigating the treacherous waters of the Puget Sound when bad weather would strike. Many storms that would beach the Coast Guard and the pirates were a walk in the park for Graignic.

By 1924, Olmstead was doing so well, he went into the wholesale business. He bought his liquor in Vancouver, British Columbia, then shipped it to Discovery Island, east of Victoria. There he sold only to reputable retailers. The business became less risky for him, and he began to enjoy the fruits of his labor. He bought a huge mansion in the prestigious Mount Baker district of Seattle, held lavish parties, and showered his personal friends, such as William Boeing, with illegal booze. He bought expensive clothes and invested in one of Seattle's first radio stations, KFQX, then later became its president and owner.

After a divorce from his first wife, Viola, he married Elise Caroline Paiche. Legend has it that she was an undercover agent, placed in Olmstead's business by the Prohibition administrator. The story is thought to be false, fueled by testimony given by Olmstead's first wife, but some prefer the irony of the legend.

Sooner or later the law was bound to catch up with Roy Olmstead. The Coast Guard started launching more boats, and it became dangerous for the liquor to be visible from the deck. Olmstead had to be more careful. He and other rum-runners had their boats outfitted with compartments below deck. Sometimes they raised suspicion when their boats rode low in the water with no cargo visible on deck, but the hidden holds were key to getting the goods to the customer. Olmstead also built a bigger, faster boat that he named *Elsie* to outrun the Coast Guard cutters. Unfortunately, one night in 1924, it caught fire and completely burned.

Sometimes Olmstead brought booze to Seattle's docks in broad daylight. His men loaded crates into trucks marked Meat, right under the noses of the Prohibition agents. He once said, "Those sons of bitches are too slow to catch cold."

Finally in 1924, Olmstead's empire came crashing down. Roy C. Lyle, Prohibition Bureau Administrator for Washington state, and William Whitney, legal advisor for the Bureau, had been putting pressure on the Coast Guard and the police to pick up the bootleggers. Whitney chartered high-speed boats to chase after them. The pressure on Olmstead increased, and so did his overhead when he had to purchase ever faster and bigger boats.

October 1924 spelled the end of Olmstead's illustrious career. His boat, the *Eva B*, was seized by Canadian officials on a customs charge. Three men and 784 cases of liquor were on board at the time. Whitney was able to extract enough information from the three men to raid Olmstead's home on November 17, 1924. Whitney also raided the office of Jerry Finch, Olmstead's attorney. On November 26, Thanksgiving morning, Prohibition agents arrested nine men, including Olmstead, Elise Olmstead, Graignic, and a King County sheriff.

After much legal maneuvering, Olmstead and ninety others were finally indicted on January 19, 1925. The charge was conspiracy to violate the Volstead Act. Also charged were George F. Reynolds and R. F. Baerman, police officers; Philip Karansky, an Olmstead associate and bootlegger in his own right; Wilbur E. Dow, customs broker; Alfred M. Hubbard, operator of Olmstead's radio station; Tom Nakagawa, Olmstead's Japanese butler; J. E. Carroll, a Tacoma garage owner; Louis and Harry Cobb, grocery store owners; and various other middlemen. Total bail for all the defendants came to about $295,000. Olmstead posted his $10,000 bail and went right back to work. He was soon placing orders for liquor like nothing had happened. But on Thanksgiving, while unloading liquor on Woodmont Beach, Olmstead was surrounded by federal agents and arrested again.

There was a long delay before his court date was set, because of the time necessary to round up all ninety defendants. Then Olmstead's attorney tried several motions to dismiss evidence. When a motion to suppress the wiretapping evidence was denied, many of Olmstead's associates panicked and fled to Canada. One of these was Graignic. Another was Dick Elbro, Olmstead's bookkeeper.

The trial finally began on January 19, 1926. Olmstead's attorney, Jerry Finch, and a man named Vanderveer represented Olmstead and twenty-nine other co-defendants. Thomas P. Revelle prosecuted the case. The state called dozens of witnesses, including Canadian officials, some of Olmstead's employees, William Boeing, and many others. One of the chief witnesses against Olmstead was Alfred Hubbard. He testified that he kept all of Olmstead's boats in tip-top condition. He also explained that he had frequently carried money for Olmstead and that he bribed certain people to look the other way.

Other witnesses included James Johnson. Once a building inspector, now a Prohibition agent, he testified about the lack of cooperation he received from certain police officers regarding the Olmstead case. Prohibition agents Earl Corwin and Russell C. Jackson also testified to witnessing several deliveries of liquor by Olmstead and others.

But at the heart of the testimony was the information obtained by the illegal wiretap. Corwin testified to hearing information regarding liquor shipments, shipping prices and schedules, and locations of boats. Prohibition agents George Behner and Claude McCrory testified to overhearing conversations between Olmstead and others. Jackson testified that he overheard Olmstead talk to Bobby Kernan about locating a missing liquor boat. E. F. Carrothers confirmed what the others had said.

Defense attorneys argued strenuously against allowing the use of the illegal wiretap as evidence. They questioned how the tappers figured they could identify individual voices of men they did not know. They objected to some testimony read from a transcript of the wiretapped conversations. The judge did dismiss some recorded conversations after Whitney's wife, who transcribed the tapes, admitted that someone else supplied the names to her. The defense successfully argued that the recorder must be able to identify who was speaking. The case had the hallmarks of a precedent-setting case. The outcome was being watched around the country, especially by law professors from the University of Washington.

Defense attorneys also argued over the admissibility of the other evidence. Olmstead's attorney, Finch, said that the papers seized from Olmstead's office and his own were illegally obtained. He acknowledged that Olmstead had once been associated with the rum trade when he purchased shares in a Canadian shipping company but claimed that he no longer had ties to it. The

Roy Olmstead, former Northwest rum king, entering the Federal Building at Seattle, Washington, to testify to a grand jury.
(Washington State Historical Society, Tacoma, Washington)

defense stated that the prosecution failed to prove there was any conspiracy among the defendants to violate the liquor laws.

Despite the efforts of the defense, Olmstead could tell the trial wasn't going in his favor. He thought that since wiretapping was illegal that the evidence would be dismissed. However, he still laughed out loud when the prosecution read the transcripts of some of the phony phone calls he used to keep the police busy. He thought it was humorous that one of the assistant U. S. attorneys was one of his best customers.

After a lengthy trial, Olmstead and twenty-one of his associates were convicted on February 20, 1926. Finch was convicted, but Olmstead's wife, Elise, was not. Ten or twelve others were released before the trial was over because their involvement was so minor. Olmstead immediately sold his house and his radio station so he could pay his legal expenses. On March 9 he was sentenced to four years' hard labor at McNeil Island Federal Penitentiary and ordered to pay an $8,000 fine. He appealed the case, but the Ninth Circuit Court of Appeals refused to hear the case. Those who were involved with Olmstead but testified against him received only one-year sentences.

After he exhausted all of his appeals, Olmstead began serving his sentence in March 1927. In February 1928, the United States Supreme Court agreed to review the case. The Supreme Court ruled that wiretapping used as evidence was not against the U.S. Constitution, though Justice Louis Brandeis wrote a dissenting opinion, agreeing that the wiretapping violated Olmstead's Fourth Amendment rights. The case became a landmark case in United States history dealing with illegal search and seizure. The case would later be overturned by Katz vs. United States in 1967.

U.S. marshals escorted Olmstead back to McNeil Island to serve the rest of his sentence. He was released on May 12, 1931. In 1935, President Franklin Roosevelt granted him a full pardon and excused him from paying his fines and court costs, an amount over $10,000.

Though many tried to get him involved in various money-making schemes, including legal importation of liquor, Olmstead rejected them all, even though he was broke. He worked for a few years as a real estate agent, then, in 1948, he became a Christian Scientist. After his conversion, he returned to McNeil Island and to the Seattle jail to preach to the prisoners there. He also operated a ministry out of a small Seattle office. His wife divorced him on May 28, 1943, claiming abandonment. He led an upstanding life until he died in 1966.

Though Olmstead was technically a criminal, many turned a blind eye to his activities. They felt that he simply supplied a commodity that many people desired and it was irrelevant that the commodity was illegal. Olmstead was a consummate businessman and always delivered what he promised. The quality and price of his merchandise could be counted on. He never committed violence during the course of his bootlegging. He didn't even allow his associates to carry weapons. He never dabbled in illegal drugs, prostitution, or gambling. Yet his case became a landmark case in the history of U.S. courts.

The 1905 Great Northern Train Robbery

On October 2, 1905, R. F. French and C. B. Martin of Ballard decided to go hunting. They left their homes about noon, intending to head north until they reached Edmonds, Washington. On their way, they encountered three rough-looking men about a mile and a half past Bitter Lake. They asked the men for directions because they weren't sure where they were, and one of the strangers responded with a muttered, "Don't know." With that, the two parties parted company. One group planned to go hunting. The other plotted to rob a train.

On the previous day at least two of that latter group had stolen a horse and buggy and had ridden to the spot where they would rob the train. They loaded the buggy full of provisions necessary for living in the outdoors. They took a few precautions before committing the crime. They didn't want the law to be able to come after them too quickly, so they cut the wires of the Independent Telephone line, as well as lines leading into Kirkland and the line linking Northrop's Landing and Medina. They drove the buggy to a place north of Ballard and left it at a secluded getaway spot. One of the men waited with the buggy; the other man walked a few miles south and waited for the train. The third man seen by the hunters was apparently not involved in the actual robbery.

About nine o'clock on the night of October 2, the Great Northern Railway No. 2 train left Seattle, heading north. As the train passed Interbay, near today's Ballard Bridge, a masked man jumped aboard the train as it sped by. He crawled to the top of the train and over the tender. Then he slipped inside the engine, startling Engineer Caulder and Fireman Julette. He ordered Caulder and Julette to keep going until they saw a campfire. Rather than risk their lives, the two men complied. They stopped the train about ten miles north of Ballard, where the robber's partner waited.

As soon as the train stopped, the partner came aboard to join the first robber, and the two thieves ordered Caulder and Julette to lead them outside to the express car. Inside the train, the passengers quickly figured out why the train had stopped, so they closed the windows and hid all their valuables. Just in case the passengers didn't think the robbers were serious, one of the robbers periodically fired shots down the length of the train to make sure no one interfered with their plan.

While the train was stopped, two other men named Frank Alfred and Roland Gibbs walked through the smoker, day coach, and tourist cars asking for contributions, claiming they had been held up and needed money to get to Spokane. Some people thought they were part of the gang holding up the train so they gave them their money. They were actually small-time hoods taking advantage of the situation to get a little free cash.

Meanwhile, the bandits broke into the express car. In those days a messenger usually rode along in the express car to protect the contents from theft. But the protection was usually not enough to thwart desperate men. Sure enough, messenger Charles Anderson hastened to follow the outlaws' orders, and he deserted his post. The bandits demanded that Julette help them blow the safe. He set the charge and lit the fuse. After the explosion, he crawled into the safe and discovered that it held no money. The robbers forced Julette to blow open a second safe. The door did not blow on the first attempt, but the second blast successfully cracked the safe door. The robbers took everything in the safe, which was mostly gold bars. Then they jumped off the train and rode their horses to the getaway buggy. In their haste, the robbers cut the hitching strap holding the horse rather than taking the time to untie it.

As soon as the robbers were out of sight, a railroad detective named M. E. Ryan called the police. Chief of Police Bennett and the night patrolman arrived about midnight to investigate the scene of the crime. Another railroad detective named M. J. Webb joined them. Deputies canvassed witnesses in the area, but no one could provide much information. One witness thought he had seen lights out on the water, a possible sign that the robbers were going to escape via Puget Sound.

Bennett found the piece of the hitching strap that the robbers had cut. He also saw a trail from a horse and buggy. One of the officers found a letter addressed to a Fred Alexander near the scene. Someone else found a .38 Colt revolver nearby.

Meanwhile, other officers interviewed the staff and passengers of the train when it reached its destination. The engineer and fireman described the two robbers, noting that one was much taller than the other. The taller one had called the other man Bill. The shorter man had called the taller man Tom. The tall one had been the person who had boarded the train and stopped it. Julette added that both men seemed to be experienced in robbing trains. No one knew exactly how much money had been in the safe, though railroad officials later stated that it was less than $1,000. A Great Northern official named Waring squelched rumors that more than $30,000 had been onboard the train.

Early the next day, Edmonds Marshal J. T. Harrison led seven men to the scene. Detectives Webb and Harrison found an abandoned horse and buggy about two and a half miles north of Bitter Lake. Inside the buggy were several switches, a pair of rubber pants, and a double-breasted, short blue overcoat lined with black and white plaid. The horse was nearly worn out and was covered with mud and foam. A damaged hitch strap hung from his neck. The detectives knew they had found the horse and buggy used by the train robbers.

After reading about the holdup in the newspaper, the two hunters, French and Martin, immediately concluded that the three men they had seen while hunting were part of the holdup gang. They described the men to the police, saying that one was about forty years old and stocky while the other two were younger, about twenty-three, with light hair and complexions. They reported having seen the three men not very far from the holdup site. After hearing their description, Marshal Harrison thought he had seen the stocky man loitering around Edmonds.

A few other witnesses came forth. Joseph French, S. A. Jones, and G. E. Ryno remembered seeing some suspicious men near and around Ballard. Farmer C. H. Thomas stated that his son had found a canvas bag with "$20,000" stenciled on it on their property.

Men scoured the area looking for the bandits. Pinkerton detectives reviewed old records and talked to ex-cons, hoping someone would turn stool pigeon. Marshal Harrison and some deputies searched the city and the wharves. Sheriff Lou Smith patrolled the Lake Washington area. He sent deputies to Bothell while he and another deputy searched the Woodinville area. He brought in a team of bloodhounds from Black Diamond to track the robbers in the dense woods. He suspected that the third man the hunters spoke of might have been involved in helping the robbers make their getaway.

Two days after the robbery, Sheriff Smith announced that he thought the robbers were none other than Bill Miner and Jake Terry. Born in Kentucky about 1847, Miner joined the army in 1864. By 1865 he was on his way to a life of crime when he stole a watch and a suit from a store. Over the course of the next forty years he made his way west, committing ever more daring crimes with a series of different partners. He spent time in prison at least twice before hooking up with Jake Terry in Washington. Born in Missouri in 1853, Terry came to Washington in the 1870s. He committed his first crime in 1873, when he shot a man in a Seattle saloon. He had already created a reputation for smuggling Chinese immigrants and opium across the international border.

The descriptions provided by Julette jibed with the known descriptions of Miner and Terry. The tall man was likely Terry, and the shorter man was probably Miner. Both men were career criminals, and both were known to have been in the area recently. At the time, Miner was at large after holding up a train in Canada. Terry was last seen living at Sumas, near the Canadian border. As far as Sheriff Smith was concerned, there was no reason to continue searching for the robbers, since he knew who they were. The Great Northern Railway posted a $5,000 reward for the capture of each of the bandits.

Jake Terry took exception to the accusation, however. He told a newspaper reporter that he was in Bellingham on the night of the holdup and in Sumas the next day. He said there was no way he could have participated in the robbery. But he

Bill Miner at San Quentin prison.
(California State Archives)

claimed he did know who did and would tell all, if only the Great Northern would treat him fairly. However, other witnesses claimed that Terry had passed through Seattle on his way to Portland. He supposedly purchased a pearl-handled revolver while in town, and Julette had noticed that one of the robbers used a pearl-handled revolver. This seemed to place Terry in the vicinity at the time of the robbery. Pinkerton detectives on the job did not believe Terry or Miner were involved, but neither did they believe that Terry knew who was.

The police continued to search for clues. Sheriff Smith tracked down Fred Alexander, the addressee of the letter found near where the train was held up. Alexander had a known partner named James L. Short. Sheriff Smith suspected that Short was involved in the train robbery when a clerk at the Seattle Hardware Company confirmed that he had recently sold a gun to Short. Sheriff Smith arrested Short, and to keep him in custody, the sheriff charged him with stealing the horse and buggy.

But no one other than Short was ever arrested for the 1905 Great Northern train robbery. Historians and lawmen claim that Bill Miner was the mastermind of the theft, in part due to his reputation as a crafty and daring robber, but the theory was never proved. He was known to have pulled two train robberies, one in Canada and one in Portland, Oregon, in much the same manner as the Great Northern robbery, but no absolute evidence linked him to the Great Northern. If he were involved, he would have been at least fifty-eight years old!

Immediately after the robbery, Miner showed up in Princeton, British Columbia, where he called himself George Edwards. He joined a man named William "Shorty" Budd, who was actually his brother. He told the townspeople that he had just returned from one of his prospecting trips.

Miner was later captured after he robbed a train in Kamloops, British Columbia on May 8, 1906. The Royal Northwest Mounted Police captured him and his accomplices a few days later. He received a life sentence but escaped prison after a few months. He remained at large for more than four years before he was captured in Georgia after a train robbery in February 1911. He escaped twice from prison in Georgia. The second time he was caught within a day, exhausted from the terrible swamp conditions and sick from drinking polluted pond water. He died a short time later on September 2, 1913, probably the most infamous train robber of his time.

Jake Terry

Jake Terry was hanging around Sumas, Washington, waiting for his next scheduled delivery when he ran into customs inspector Lawrence J. Flanigan, who was trying to catch him in the act of smuggling. He bragged to Flanigan that he would be crossing the border between Washington and British Columbia with illegal Chinese immigrants that night and that there was no way Flanigan would catch him. He was so sure of himself that he even told Flanigan where he was planning to cross the border.

"Terrible Terry's" attitude made Flanigan ever more determined to catch him. He deputized A. Schumaker to help him, and the two men borrowed a railroad speeder, a hand-driven railroad car, and rode to the spot where Terry had said he would cross. They left the speeder parked on the track, where it would be in Terry's way, and hid out of sight.

Meanwhile, Terry picked up his contraband—four Chinese illegal aliens. The Chinese Exclusion Act of 1882 barred Chinese immigrants from entering the United States. Only those who had immigrated before November 17, 1880, could remain in America. Demand for their cheap labor was still very high, however, and Washington state was in an advantageous location for a lucrative smuggling trade. Human contraband could be smuggled in by land and by water. Terry was one of many who profited from transporting Chinese immigrants.

That day, Terry and the four Chinese immigrants boarded a railroad handcar in Canada, and Terry propelled them down the line. About two o'clock the next morning, Terry arrived at the speeder blocking his way. The Chinese men began to panic, but Terry kept his cool. Before he could think of a plan, however, Flanigan and Schumaker, the customs men, jumped out of their hiding place and demanded his surrender. Terry did as he was told. He didn't even get a chance to draw his own gun. The jig was up.

Flanigan marched him into town and threw him in the city jail. He was held on bail of $2,000. He did not have the money so he had to stay in jail until his trial. Originally the trial was set for March 9, 1894, but Terry waived his right to a speedy trial, choosing instead to go to the district court in Seattle. His trial began on June 5. He pled guilty to the charge of smuggling and was sentenced to one year in prison and a $1,000 fine.

Born in Missouri in 1853, Terry had come to Washington sometime in the 1870s. He committed his first crime on July 19, 1873, when he had an argument with Delbert Wright, proprietor of the Fashion Saloon in Seattle. Terry did not want to pay for his drinks. Wright insisted that Terry pay his bill. Terry left the saloon but came right back with a gun and wounded Wright in the chest.

Two days later Terry was arrested for assault. On August 5 he was found guilty. He appealed the conviction, but the decision was upheld. He was sentenced to five years at the territorial penitentiary in Steilacoom. He was released in August 1878.

He left the state for the next few years and worked as a railroad engineer. Perhaps Terry meant to stay out of trouble, but while running a train across the Canadian border, he realized he had a lucrative opportunity to smuggle illegal Chinese immigrants into the United States. After several successful runs, he started attracting too much attention, so he decided to move on. On his way back west, he stopped in Montana. He met a woman there named Annie, whom he brought back to Washington with him. They moved to Island County in 1883 or 1884 and lived together for five years before they split up. What Terry did for a living during that time is unknown, but presumably he kept on smuggling.

He moved to Seattle after his breakup with Annie, and for a while he drove a stage between Cherry Street and Ravenna Park, making one trip every hour. After that he worked as pound master of the city. He also served a short stint as a police officer but was fired because his bosses didn't like the company he kept—or perhaps the activities he engaged in, such as counterfeiting. He left Seattle proper and settled in Kellytown, a small town outside of Seattle.

Soon Terry returned to smuggling. In July 1891, he made plans to smuggle some Chinese across the border near Sumas. He traveled on foot from his home to Sedro. From there he sent a telegram to Zachary Holden, an unscrupulous customs inspector from Seattle. Holden and Deputy Marshal George Poor met Terry at Sedro. Terry knew from experience on the Seattle police force that he could count on both men to assist him in his scheme.

Meanwhile, two other customs inspectors had heard rumors of the plan, so they met near Sedro to try to intercept the smugglers and their contraband. On about July 26, the customs inspectors ran into Holden and Poor in Sedro. To avert suspicion, Holden told them that he and Poor had heard that illegal Chinese immigrants were in the area and that they were looking for them.

Something in his remarks or attitude told one of the customs inspectors that all was not right, so he followed Poor until he met with Terry, who was leading about fifteen Chinese men. The customs inspector saw them and ordered them to surrender, but Poor declared he was a U.S. marshal and had come to arrest Terry himself. The customs inspector didn't believe him and ordered both men to raise their hands. No one knows who went for their gun first, but Poor was soon dead and Terry was injured. The immigrants scattered and were never found.

The customs men carried Terry to town, where a doctor examined him. The doctor predicted that Terry didn't have long to live, so officers took what they thought would be a deathbed statement. Terry stated that he warned King County Sheriff Woolery about some Chinese being smuggled and stated he could capture them if Woolery sent help. Poor and Holden were the men Woolery sent. They had simply been taking the Chinese to the authorities, he claimed.

Terry survived his injuries and was soon charged with smuggling Chinese laborers into the United States. He was held on $1,500 bail. His trial was scheduled for December. While awaiting trial he was sent to the McNeil Island Penitentiary. He tried to escape with four others on October 11, but they were captured the next day.

Terry went to trial on December 15, and the jury found him guilty of smuggling Chinese laborers into the United States. He was sentenced to ten months at McNeil Island and required to pay court costs. Because he had no money, the court ordered that his personal possessions be sold to pay the court costs of $550.60. After discovering that Terry had nothing to sell, the judge added thirty days to his sentence.

Initially the two customs inspectors were also arrested for killing Poor. They were tried and convicted for manslaughter but were later released because both had acted "in good faith." Terry testified at their hearing, stating that the officers had fired first and that he had had no gun with which to defend himself. Terry's statement was largely ignored.

On December 23, 1891, Terry was taken to McNeil Island to serve his sentence. He was released early on September 30, 1892 for good behavior. But Terry had not learned his lesson; he went back to smuggling immediately. He set up his headquarters at Sumas, a perfect location for getting men across the border easily and quickly under cover of night. On May 30, 1893, he smuggled three men across the border and put them on the Whatcom train with no questions asked.

Terry enjoyed playing jokes on his pursuers. One particularly memorable trick was one he played on customs inspector Flanigan. One day Flanigan boarded the train at Sumas after receiving a tip that opium would be smuggled on that train. He spotted a package taped underneath one of the railroad cars. He ripped the box off the railroad car and took it to the station agent. After some struggle, he finally got the box open. His mouth fell open in shock when he saw its contents—horse manure! No doubt, Terry himself was the source of the opium rumor!

Flanigan turned the tables on him though, when Terry bragged about where he would cross the border with his illegal immigrants. This incident would once again land him at McNeil Island Penitentiary. He was released early for good behavior on May 24, 1895.

Yet another prison term did not set him straight. He did realize that he would probably be watched closely for a while, so he tried his hand at the less visible crime of counterfeiting.

He and his partner, Dave Dixon, set up a shop on Camano Island where they made fake silver ten-cent coins. Terry gave thirty of the coins to a woman on the island. Shortly afterward, he was arrested by U.S. Deputy Marshal James M. Quilter. Quilter took him to Everett for a preliminary hearing. Bail was set at $2,500. Once again, Terry had no money, so he had to stay at the King County jail until his trial in December.

As bad luck would have it, the same judge presided over this trial as his earlier one. Judge Cornelius Hanford labeled him a career criminal and this time sentenced him to ten years of hard labor at McNeil Island Penitentiary.

On December 26, 1895, Terry and five others were transferred to the infamous San Quentin prison in California after U.S. Marshal James C. Drake petitioned the attorney general to allow transfer of some convicts to a more secure prison. Again Terry behaved himself while in prison and was released early on June 2, 1902. While behind bars he met someone who would become his next partner in crime—Bill Miner. Miner had been in prison almost twenty years when he was released a year before Terry. Miner was living in Bellingham with his sister when Terry was released in 1902, and Terry joined Miner there.

In 1904, Terry and Miner decided to rob a train in British Columbia. Neither had robbed a train before, but Terry's experience as a railroad engineer came in handy. Terry found out that a gold shipment was on its way to Seattle. In September, Miner and his partner Shorty Dunn left Miner's home in Princeton, British Columbia, telling townspeople they were off on a hunting trip. A short while later, they met up with Terry near the Canadian border.

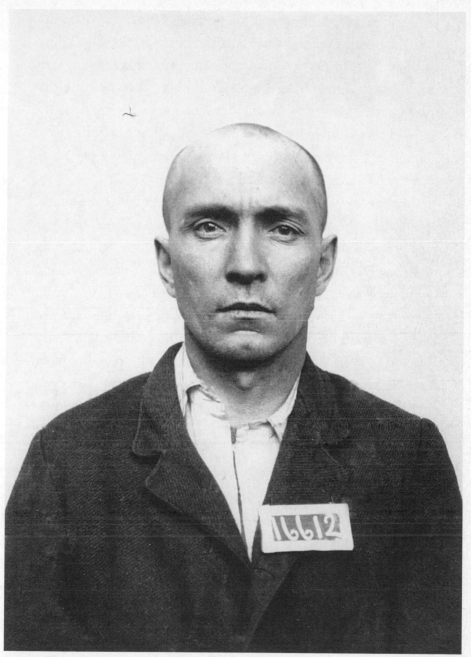

Jake Terry at San Quentin prison, approximately 1896.
(California State Archives)

At about half past nine on the night of September 10, 1904, the three men boarded the Canadian Pacific Railway Transcontinental Express No. 1 at Mission Junction, about forty miles east of Vancouver, British Columbia. They hid until the train gathered speed, then they crawled over the roofs of the railroad cars until they reached the engine. They held Engineer Nathaniel J. Scott and Fireman Harry Freeman at gunpoint and told them to stop the train.

Miner ordered Freeman to uncouple the express car from the rest of the train. Then he ordered the engineer to pull the train forward to the Whonock milepost and stop. Terry guarded the fireman while Miner and Dunn led Scott back to the express car. Opening the safe should have been a piece of cake. Earlier in the day, Terry had sent a telegraph to the train station, pretending to be a railroad official. He claimed that the combination to the safe had been lost and asked that the safe be left open. But when Terry checked the safe, nothing was in it. All was not lost, however—there was another safe. Miner commanded the express messenger, Herb Mitchell, to open it. Mitchell did as he was told. Six thousand dollars in gold dust and $1,000 in cash were stored in the second safe. Miner also took $50,000 in U.S. bonds and about $250,000 in Australian securities from the registered mail.

The crime was the first train robbery in Canadian history, so British Columbia police had no experience to guide their investigations. They asked the Pinkerton Detective Agency for help. The Pinkertons were sure that Bill Miner was involved, but they couldn't prove it. After a short investigation, they gave up the hunt.

Terry and Miner found out that Miner was the chief suspect. They also knew that as soon as they cashed the bonds their trail could be traced. The wisest course of action was to part ways. Terry returned to Bellingham, where he supposedly spent October 2, 1905, the night of the Great Northern train robbery, in Seattle. A reward of $1,000 was offered for the capture of the bandits who robbed the Great Northern train, but the perpetrators were never caught. Even so, the robbery was always attributed to Terry, Miner, and Dunn.

After that, Terry moved his headquarters to Port Townsend. He started smuggling again, but in December of 1905 he returned to Sumas for Christmas. He just happened to walk into a notions store and found that the proprietor was none other than his ex-wife Annie.

After her breakup with Terry back in 1889, Annie had stayed on in Sumas and opened the store. The store sold such items as cigars, candy, and writing materials. Annie was very popular and every man in town wanted to court her. Finally she accepted the attentions of a man named Gus Linday, a telegraph lineman. When he asked her to marry him, she said yes. They set up a home in the back rooms of her shop.

Terry was overjoyed to see her, but he did not realize she was married. While Terry talked to her, the very jealous Linday walked in and let Terry know how things stood. Terry backed off but noted that Annie didn't seem to be in overwhelming agreement with her husband. Her hesitation encouraged Terry to pursue the issue right then and there. Soon the two men were throwing punches. Finally Terry had the upper hand and threw Linday out of the house. Linday returned the next day, but Terry threw him out again.

Linday went across the street and drowned his sorrows with a few drinks. Two days later he led some men to the store intending to reclaim his wife. Before they could approach the door, Terry fired at the group from inside. Linday and everybody else scattered. Terry strolled down the street after them, firing shots over their heads. For nearly a week Terry terrorized the town, shooting at anyone in his way.

The sheriff arrested Terry a few days later and escorted him to the county seat at Bellingham. He was held on $250 bail, but Annie paid the bond almost immediately. Terry didn't stand around waiting for his hearing. Because Sumas was so close to the Canadian border, Terry skedaddled over the line and set up new smuggling operations in the Huntington Hotel. By crossing the border, Terry forfeited his bail. A warrant was immediately issued for his arrest, but as long as he stayed in Canada he was beyond the reach of American lawmen.

Terry began smuggling opium across the border. The drug was in high demand by the Chinese immigrants already living in the United States. Though lawmen dogged him at every step, they were not able to catch him. They even set traps for him, to no avail. When he needed money, Terry would work as a logger or an engineer. George Manning, an immigration guard, passed notes back and forth across the border for Terry and Annie, and Terry gave Annie money, probably part of the booty from the train robberies. It was only a matter of time before Terry had another showdown with Gus Linday.

On July 5, 1907, Terry snuck back across the border. After having a few drinks at the Sumas saloon, he walked down the block to Annie's store. He confronted Linday, who ordered him to leave their house. Terry refused. Annie saw trouble brewing and ran for the sheriff. By the time she returned, Terry was dead from two gunshot wounds to his head and side.

Immediately Linday ran down the street to the judge's office and turned himself in. He had attracted so much sympathy among the townspeople that Sumas merchants practically fought each other to post Linday's bail of $7,000. George Bocking, Frank Hayworth, C. E. Moulton, D. B. Lucas, and William Gerstberger put up the money, and Linday was released. He returned to his job on the telegraph line and divorced Annie, who left Sumas and was never seen again.

On the day of the murder, Terry's body was taken to the Gillies Hardware Store. People came to gawk, and, incredibly, his autopsy was performed right there in the store window, where anyone could watch. After the formalities were over, Terry's body was shipped to Bellingham and buried in a potter's field.

Over the course of fifteen years, Terry was the terror of Puget Sound. Whether he was robbing trains, smuggling Chinese men or opium, or counterfeiting, he led police officers on quite a chase. In the end, the law couldn't catch up with him, but a jealous husband did. Gus Linday ended Terrible Terry's reign as king of the smugglers with two well-placed shots from his gun.

Billy Gohl

Constable George Dean sat quietly in his office wondering how he was going to catch the man responsible for the murders committed near the Wishkah and Chehalis Rivers in southwestern Washington. Suddenly, a messenger burst in with news that another body had turned up. Other victims had been found moving on the river currents and had been dubbed "floaters." This one was no different. Dean left his office to check it out.

The body was taken to the coroner's office, where Dean looked it over for clues. The victim had no special physical characteristics, but he did carry an unusual gold pocketwatch inscribed "Otto Kurtz." The watch alone might be enough to identify him. As usual, Dean called Billy Gohl, head of the Sailor's Union, for help in identifying the body. Gohl had performed this service many times in the past since sailors registered with his office when they came into port.

Gohl did not know the man's name, but he did recognize him. He had visited the union hall two weeks earlier with a friend to pay his dues. Gohl volunteered to contact the friend to see what he could find out. Gohl did not know that Dean knew about the pocketwatch. The next day Gohl returned and told Dean that the dead man's friend had left town, but he had been able to find out that the man's name was Otto Kurtz. He was from Goerlitz, Germany. Dean thanked Gohl for his time as the wheels started turning in his mind.

Dean had not told Gohl that he recognized the dead man, too. Two weeks earlier, this man had asked Dean about boardinghouses in the area. Dean had recommended a particular boardinghouse, so he decided to see if the man had taken his recommendation. He described the dead man to the landlady. She knew him as Rudolph Alterman, one of her boarders. She hadn't seen him for a week. He had gone to pay his union dues, she said, and hadn't returned. When the two searched Alterman's room, Dean found a photo of the man and some mail addressed to Rudolph Alterman.

Dean now knew the identity of the victim. He also discovered that the name on the watch was not the name of the owner, but the name of the maker! He wrote to the company and found that the person who had purchased that watch was named Fred Nielssen, a Danish seaman. Dean figured the only way Gohl could have known the name Otto Kurtz was if he too had seen the man's pocketwatch. Dean suspected he now knew the identity of the killer. He doubled his efforts toward finding a way to prove Gohl's guilt.

Gohl had committed other crimes long before he came to Aberdeen, Washington. Born in Germany on February 6, 1873, he had come to Washington via Alaska and San Francisco. He fled Alaska when he became the prime suspect in the murder of his mining partner. He showed up in San Francisco, where he joined the Sailor's Union of the Pacific. While there, he learned that a ship employing non-union labor was trying to take over the union port. Gohl told union leaders he would take care of the problem. The union didn't question his methods—they just gave him some money to cover any expenses he incurred. Gohl learned the name of one of the sailors aboard the non-union ship and pretended to be a friend of this man so he could gain access to the ship. When he was led to the man, he held his "friend" at gunpoint then coerced each of the crew members to disembark. He marched all the sailors to the union hall, where they were dealt with. Gohl's reputation for hardheadedness was established.

In 1902 Gohl moved to Aberdeen, Washington. Whether he went there for some purpose or if he traveled there just by happenstance is unknown. Aberdeen was a rough town of about twelve thousand people at the time. Gohl opened a cigar store at 313 1⁄2 South F Street and rented a room at a nearby boardinghouse on East First Street. He worked the cigar store by day and became a crimper at night. A crimper was a thug of sorts who forced or entrapped men into service as sailors, a practice also known as shanghaiing. Whenever a ship was a few sailors short of a crew, Gohl visited saloons to look for likely candidates. He slipped a "mickey"—a knockout drug—into a man's drink or waited until he passed out on his own. Then he dragged him out of the saloon and helped himself to the man's cash before leaving him onboard ship. When the man woke up, he was likely far out to sea with no way back to shore. As an added bonus, Gohl received a stipend from the ship's captain for each sailor he "recruited."

Gohl managed to get himself appointed a shop steward of the Sailor's Union of the Pacific. He set up an office on the wharf, in the second floor of the Grand Saloon at 300 South F Street. The front of the building faced the street, and the back rested on a dock on the west bank of the Wishkah River. It was a perfect location from which to conduct his business.

Round-headed, broad-shouldered, and barrel-chested, Billy Gohl parted his hair in the middle like many bartenders of the day. He spoke with a slight German accent. His appearance was boyish, and he was very charming. His charm overcame a dance hall girl named Bessie Hager, and they were married on May 16, 1905. Evidently she was a bit rough herself. She either didn't care about Gohl's true character or was naive. She would be his staunchest supporter when the law finally caught up with him

By 1906, Gohl had Aberdeen in his grip. Virtually everyone in town either feared or admired him. The sailors admired him for his guts and hardheadedness because he helped them in many ways. He knew multiple languages, so he often helped the international sailors by acting as their interpreter. He loaned a sailor a few dollars if he had been robbed while drunk. Sailors trusted him to keep their money in his safe while they were in port. He defended sailors who were in trouble because he disliked the area's capitalists and lumber barons. The wealthy citizens of the town didn't like him because he could cripple their operations by taking union men out on strike. Gohl repeatedly threatened to burn down the business of anyone who defied him.

Despite his apparent loyalty to the sailors, Gohl committed his greatest crimes against them. The captain of the ship *Fearless* did not want to hire union sailors. The boat sailed out of the harbor with the two non-union men, "scabs," aboard. Gohl wouldn't hear of it. He gathered some friends, and they set sail in a launch without lights so the schooner couldn't see them. Gohl and his men boarded the schooner and demanded that the captain turn over the two non-union men. The captain, C. W. Lilliquist, wasn't going to just give in. When he ordered them off his ship, Billy opened fire. When a man was killed, the captain released the two men to avoid further bloodshed. Gohl took them back to Aberdeen.

Gohl was arrested almost immediately. He was tried and convicted on a charge of piracy. He appealed the decision, but the charge was upheld by the state supreme court. Instead of a long prison term, he was fined $1,200. The union paid his fine.

But these were petty crimes compared to what Gohl did next. He used his position of authority with the union to lure the sailors into a false sense of security. When a sailor came to pick up his paycheck or mail or stash his valuables, Gohl allowed the man to place his belongings in a cubbyhole in his safe. When the sailor turned his back, Gohl clubbed him over the head. Sometimes the blow was enough to kill the man outright. Sometimes it only knocked him unconscious. In either case, it was enough for Gohl to get what he wanted. He pocketed the man's valuables for himself.

When the time was right, he disposed of the body. The rear of the building hung out over the water, so sometimes he dropped the body through a trapdoor in the floor straight into the water. Other times, he kept a small rowboat tied to the pier beneath the building. He dropped the body into the rowboat, then after dark he rowed the boat out into deep water and dumped the body overboard. If the sailor was not already dead, dumping him into the harbor made sure that he would not live to identify Gohl.

Once in a while he almost capsized his boat getting a body out of it. A few times a body got stuck on a pier or washed into the tide flats because he could not row out far enough. Finally, he bought a gas-powered launch with his ill-gotten gains, so he could tow the rowboat farther out into the harbor. When he was far enough out, he tipped the rowboat over by pulling on its towrope.

When the bodies were found, the police often called Gohl to identify them because he had so much contact with sailors through the union. Usually he could provide a name and a few bucks for a burial. He would tell the union that he had forwarded the rest of the sailor's pay to the victim's family. Of course, he had already pocketed the money himself.

Though sailors were Gohl's main targets, many others suffered at his hand. Anyone who crossed him would know his wrath. Many of his crimes were against men who dared to oppose him in business. Others he appeared to target just for the fun of it. On May 5, 1906, the body of J. B. Mears was found in the Wishkah River. Mears was a timber cruiser for the Continental Timber Company. A timber cruiser selected and marked appropriate trees for harvesting. The man was last seen making the rounds of some Aberdeen saloons. He was known to have had about $700 in cash, but it was not found on his body. The money likely disappeared into Gohl's pocket.

In 1906 the Slade Mill's union workers were threatening to strike. W. B. Mack, the manager of the mill, refused to meet their demands, so Gohl threatened to blow up the mills. He planted bombs, but the one at Slade Mill did not detonate.

Another one of Gohl's targets was the Brunswick Hotel. Gohl had an ongoing dispute with Lee Williams, proprietor of the hotel's Alaska Saloon. Gohl bragged that he would get even with Williams. And he did. He burned the hotel and saloon to the ground. Fortuitously for Gohl, another old enemy, George Griswold, happened to be staying at the hotel and died in the fire. Supposedly Gohl said of the incident, "Ain't it funny how things work out? I never dreamed there'd be a bonus in it."

Gohl was suspected as the criminal behind the fire, but there was no way to prove he was responsible.

Gohl also controlled a group of henchmen who did his bidding. He instructed his henchmen to rob ships while they were in port. Others set up a protection racket, extracting cuts from local brothels and saloons. He and his gang routinely shanghaied sailors for ship captains whose crews were a little short. Sometimes his crew would drill holes in the bottom of a ship and plug them with tallow. When the tallow worked itself free, the ship would fill up with water and sink.

One of his tactics was to substitute his own henchmen for skilled sailors. The unsuspecting captain would hire these men from Gohl's roster. As soon as the regular crew was asleep or ashore, Gohl's henchmen would sneak around the ship and steal instruments, money, food, and anything else of value. Then they would desert the ship and row away. Gohl would "come to the rescue" of the poor captain who had been robbed and give him some real union sailors. The captain would be in such a hurry to leave port, so that he wouldn't be robbed again, that he wouldn't take the time to report the crime.

Michael McCarron, captain of the *Sophie Christenson*, was one of the few to outwit Gohl. He didn't like the way Gohl ran his union shop, so he thought he'd have a little fun with him. He had just finished loading a boat with timber from a mill on the Wishkah River. The boat was rather large for the river and the channel, so it was towed back out to the bay by a tug. When the *Sophie Christenson* was abreast of the union hall, the captain steered the boat straight toward the hall. The boat's long jib boom knocked the hall's privy right off its foundation. As the boat moved on, the "two-holer" hung right there on the boom.

The crew and onlookers were much amused by this. McCarron let the lavatory hang there until he was some distance out in the harbor, where he finally dumped it. McCarron declared that it wasn't his fault, it must have been the tug or the current. He was hailed as a hero by his friends. Gohl was not amused.

Little else seemed to threaten Gohl at all. In July 1907, while performing one of his dirty deeds, he punctured the middle finger of his left hand. The wound became infected, and soon he was sick with blood poisoning. Even then, however, luck saved Gohl. Surgery saved his arm, and he was able to fight the infection. Soon he was up and about and as good as new.

Gohl seemed to be especially active in 1907, judging by the many bodies found in the nearby waters. The first victim that year was Askel Johnson, found on February 8. Just a week later, someone found John Anderson, a native of Finland, near the Wilson mill. In April, the bodies of Gus Lindros and Robert Priest were found. He struck again in May, when he killed Connie Lockett. In June, the body of Gabriel Austad, a Norwegian logger, was found.

He definitely had a cruel streak too. One night that year, Gohl left four scab sailors on Moon Island during an incoming tide, knowing they would surely die. He laughed when the men claimed they couldn't swim. Another time, after a sailor had deposited his money with Gohl, Gohl told him to wait on the docks for a boat. When darkness fell, Gohl shot the man in the head. He waited until boat whistles masked the noise of his gun. Gohl kept the sailor's $200.

Ralph Peasley, an old sea captain and the leader of some non-union workers, managed the Grays Harbor Ship Chandlery. Peasley had been trying to break a longshoremen's strike led by Gohl. He paid dearly for his trouble. On June 11, 1909, Gohl set fire to the Zelasko building on East Wishkah between F and G Streets. The Zelasko building housed the Chandlery on the ground floor.

About the same time another man was found dead in the middle of F Street. Gohl bragged about shooting him from inside his office. Shortly after that, Gohl was arrested for stealing two blankets from a car, but one of his henchmen, Charles Hadberg, claimed he bought them from a pawn shop and gave them to Gohl.

Gohl managed to escape detection for his crimes mostly because of the location of his office. His office was surrounded by businesses that were only open during the day. No one was around at night to witness any of his unsavory deeds. On the wharf on the opposite side of the river was the Harbor Produce company. Vegetables were delivered early in the morning, but no one was there at night. Next door were a saloon, a restaurant, an employment agency, and Frank M. Potter's store. Only the saloon was open at night, and none of the patrons paid much attention to anything happening at Gohl's office. A blacksmith shop and a fire station also provided cover noise. Often times, Gohl just waited for a fire alarm and took care of business during all the commotion. One rumor says that henchman Hadberg deliberately set fires to cause a commotion when Gohl needed a distraction.

By 1910, Gohl's crime wave was giving Aberdeen a bad reputation. The city became known as the "port of missing men," and people said that it had a "floater fleet." Most of the victims were sailors and lumberjacks. Those who checked into hotels in town were nervous that they might become victims, so they started going to nearby Hoquiam to spend their money. Business in Aberdeen flagged. The city fathers wanted to stop the killings. The new mayor, Ed Benn, appointed George Dean, of Cosmopolis, the chief of police. Dean's top priority was to clean up the town. Dean raised $10,000 from mill owners and businessmen to trap and capture the notorious Billy Gohl. With the money, Dean hired two detectives from the famous Thiel Agency. Dean installed Detective Paddy McHugh in the Grand Saloon as a bartender to keep an eye on the comings and goings of Gohl, who conducted his business upstairs.

The incident with the Otto Kurtz pocketwatch caused Dean to watch Gohl more closely. Then Detective McHugh told Dean about an incident at a remote farm at Lone Tree Point. Apparently a teenage girl had been raped and the family's livestock had been run off. Dean had not noticed a report of the crime in the local paper, so he decided to investigate himself. When he talked to the family, they tried to deny that the incident had occurred, but Dean noticed that some of the cattle they used to own were no longer on the farm. He questioned the farmer again, and the man admitted what had happened but said he did not want anyone to know about it.

Gohl heard that Dean had been to the farm and figured that someone must have tipped off Dean about the incident. He suspected McHugh and questioned him. McHugh didn't want to blow his cover, so he put up a good front, suggesting that the stool pigeon must have been one of Gohl's two close friends—either John Hoffman or Charles Hadberg. McHugh pretended that he could never tell on Gohl because Gohl knew too much of his past, but that was just a ploy he made up to get into Gohl's good graces. Gohl let McHugh off the hook and turned his attention to the other two men. Unfortunately, that attention meant a death sentence for Hoffman and Hadberg.

For a time Gohl was moody and morose. He would barely talk to anybody. Then about Christmastime, he seemed to perk up. Shortly after Christmas, Gohl came into the saloon already drunk. McHugh and the other undercover detective named Billie Montana sat down with Gohl and pretended to get drunk with him. McHugh casually mentioned that he had not seen Hoffman or Hadberg or another Gohl henchman, John Klingenberg, lately. He wondered if they hadn't returned to Europe, as they were all immigrants. Gohl's comment was, "They went away for good." Later that night McHugh reported Gohl's remark to Dean.

Gohl's mood had improved because Hadberg, Hoffman, and Klingenberg had been "dealt with." On December 20, Gohl sent one of his henchmen over to Klingenberg's house. The message said he should meet Gohl at the union hall that night. When Klingenberg arrived, Gohl told him his plans for dealing with the two other men. Klingenberg tried to dissuade him, but Gohl wasn't listening. On their way to Hadberg's home they picked up Hoffman. The three of them went to visit Hadberg.

They rowed down the Chehalis River to the mouth of Indian Creek, where Hadberg lived in a cabin that actually belonged to Gohl. It was one of several that he maintained as hideouts for his goons. On the way to Hadberg's house, Gohl ruthlessly and without warning shot Hoffman. Then he ordered Klingenberg to tie an anchor to him, and the two men tossed the body over the side of the boat. They continued rowing toward Indian Creek; Gohl acted as if absolutely nothing unusual had happened.

At Hadberg's cabin the three men shared a meal and bunked down for the night. The three woke the next morning and had a light breakfast. Then Gohl persuaded Hadberg to leave Indian Creek with them. Gohl sat in the stern of the boat, while Klingenberg sat in the bow. Hadberg was between them, with his back to Klingenberg. After they reached the harbor, Gohl directed Klingenberg to shoot Hadberg. Klingenberg didn't want to do it, but Gohl threatened to kill them both if he did not. So Klingenberg shot Hadberg, and they weighed his body with the boat anchor and tossed him over the side. They also dumped three guns, a tool case, and a suitcase full of clothes into the water.

The two rowed back to town. Gohl was unruffled and cool. That would teach those no-goods to fink on him, he thought. Klingenberg was afraid for his life. As soon as possible, he boarded a schooner headed for Mexico. He figured that was far enough away to be beyond Gohl's reach.

As soon as McHugh reported what Gohl had said about the men having "gone away," Dean began investigating. He searched Hadberg's cabin but could not find any evidence of a crime. Dean asked some volunteers from the Oddfellow's Lodge to look for the three missing men. They posed as fishermen while they searched, in case Gohl was watching. Finally brothers George and William Lightfoot found Hadberg's body on February 3, 1910, near the mouth of Indian Creek. A fifty-pound anchor was tied to his back, and he had two bullet wounds in his head. Three guns, a case full of clothes, and a tool case were near the body.

This time Gohl had miscalculated. The tide had been in when he dropped Hadberg's body over the side of the boat.

When the tide went out again, the body was exposed, trapped in the mud. Dean and another man rowed out to the site.

The next day Dean sent a detective to Gohl's office to bring him to Dean's office. When he arrived, Dean arrested Gohl for Hadberg's murder and held him without bail. After dark he was taken to the county jail at Montesano. As soon as Gohl's regular attorney, Wilson Buttner, saw the evidence against his client, he resigned. Gohl's wife claimed he was innocent, and she brought him food and books and even weapons for a breakout.

Meanwhile, Dean continued looking for Klingenberg and Hoffman. After investigating, Dean found that Klingenberg had sailed on the ship *A. J. Ness*. He sent a telegraph to the ship's captain, and as instructed by Dean, the captain prevented Klingenberg from leaving the ship. When his business in Mexico was finished, the captain returned to Grays Harbor. There he turned Klingenberg over to Deputy Sheriff Schelle Mathews.

Mathews escorted Klingenberg to the county jail. He broke down and told everything he knew, saying that he had not had a good night's sleep since the incident. He said he would wake up with the faces of the dead men in his head. He would hear Hoffman begging, "For God's sake, don't kill me, Billy, don't kill me."

Lauritz Jentzen, known as "The Weasel," was also arrested about the same time. He told Dean about many of Gohl's past crimes, including an incident when Gohl shot a sailor from his office window because the sailor had been on his blacklist. He related that Gohl had set the fire that burned down the Zelasko block because of a grudge Gohl held against the owner. He also told how Gohl burned down Lee Williams's saloon and how he robbed Frank Becker's store.

Gohl hired an attorney named A. M. Abel. The lawyer had an office near Gohl, so Abel knew who Gohl was. He was aware of Gohl's reputation but felt the man should be defended if there was any chance of doubt. The trial was originally scheduled for March 25, 1910, but Abel filed a motion for a new date so he could prepare Gohl's defense. The court granted his motion. But before deciding if he would represent Gohl, Abel visited him in the county jail at Montesano. To his amazement, Gohl bragged about the many crimes he had committed. At first Abel thought he was lying. But Gohl continued to brag about what he had done and expressed certainty that his friends would break him out of jail.

Abel couldn't believe the gall of the man, but he did believe that Gohl's boast about the jailbreak was true. Gohl already had a knife and a gun that his friends had snuck in to him. Abel tried to remain unaffected long enough to get out of the jail with his own skin intact. He said he would be in touch and warned Gohl not to do anything foolish. As a parting shot, Gohl told him that the union would be putting up $50,000 for his defense so he could easily pay Abel's fee.

Abel knew his conscience wouldn't allow him to defend Gohl. He reported what he had seen and heard to Judge Mason Irwin. The judge told him he had acted correctly in telling him because client confidentiality did not apply if another crime was about to be committed. He ordered Sheriff Ed Payette to search Gohl's cell, who found the gun and knife and other forbidden items.

Gohl's trial began on May 2, 1910, before Judge Ben Sheeks. The union never came through with any money, so Gohl was represented by two public defenders named J. A. Hutcheson and A. E. Cross. William E. Campbell and E. E. Boner represented the state. It took three days passed to select an impartial. In the end, many of the jurors lived in the eastern part of the county, where Gohl was less notorious.

The state called forty-nine witnesses, including Paddy McHugh. He said he heard Gohl threaten to kill Hoffman and Hadberg.

Constable Dean produced the automatic pistol that had been found under Hadberg's body. The defense said it was not Hadberg's body. But the state produced a piece of evidence that laid the matter to rest—a piece of skin from the body that had a peculiar tattoo. Emil Olson, a friend of Hadberg, had given him the tattoo. He said it concealed a scar from a knife fight.

Klingenberg also testified for the state. He explained how, on December 20, 1909, Gohl had met with him and told him of his plans. He described how Gohl killed Hoffman. He explained his own part in the murder of Hadberg.

The trial lasted nine days. The jury deliberated for nine hours. On May 12, the jury foreman, L. O. Stewart, announced the guilty verdict. Though he did not pull the trigger himself, Gohl was found guilty of aiding and abetting the murder of Hadberg. Though he did kill Hoffman, he was not charged for this murder because the body was never recovered. On May 24, Judge Sheeks sentenced Gohl to life in prison. Klingenberg was tried in October. Though there were extenuating circumstances, Klingenberg was also convicted of murder. He received the lesser sentence of fifteen years. He was later released and went on to lead a productive life.

The number of murders Billy Gohl committed varies from report to report. One source "credits" Gohl with 124 deaths, including only those that were found in the water. Forty-three of Gohl's murders were committed during an eight-month period. Some estimates say that he may have killed as many as two hundred men. Most were merchant seamen. Dean always believed Gohl had killed many more than just those that were found, but the only crime for which he was convicted was the death of Hadberg.

After a few years in the state prison, Gohl began to show signs of instability. He witnessed the stabbing of an inmate and, for some reason, was deeply troubled by the sight. Supposedly the crime sickened him because he never used a knife himself, only a gun, a club, or his hands. He was transferred to the Eastern State Hospital at Medical Lake, near Spokane, Washington, where he died March 3, 1927. His death certificate listed lobar pneumonia, erysilpelas, and dementia paralytic (a mental disorder resulting from syphilis) as the causes of death.

The Cashmere Fence Dispute

Della Tabor, recently widowed, moved to Washington state about 1900. She brought with her a herd of goats and her twelve-year-old son, Will Tabor. She first settled in Ellensburg but she could not make a success of her goat business there. She herded the goats north and settled in the Wenatchee River valley at the end of Brender Canyon, about five miles southwest of Cashmere, Washington.

For a few years, she made a living from the goats. After a while she grew crops when the goat herd no longer provided enough income. After a few years, her mother, Hannah Beebe, bought the adjoining property. Between them, they blazed roads from their properties to the nearby railroad line. They also planted fruit trees.

Having more people move to such a remote area would make most homesteaders feel safer. But for some reason Mrs. Tabor had a problem with her new neighbors, the Suttons, almost from the moment they moved in. Their initial disagreements arose out of misunderstandings about the roads. After one such dispute, James Sutton, the patriarch of the family, retaliated by cutting down a fence and letting Mrs. Tabor's goats get loose. He also may have been the one who sent her an anonymous threatening letter.

Another time, somebody climbed on top of her roof during the night. She grabbed her shotgun and quietly went upstairs. She listened carefully to the footsteps on the roof and when she thought she was directly under them, she fired through the roof. All of a sudden the footsteps scrambled down and ran away.

She fired after the fleeing figure but could not see who it was. She felt sure it was someone in the Sutton family harassing her.

Della Tabor married Noel Totten in 1909. He tried to settle the problems with the Sutton family and was making headway when the Sutton brothers stirred up trouble again. Mrs. Totten had them arrested for disturbing the peace in June 1910. At that time, Jim Sutton was reprimanded for making loud remarks to Mrs. Totten. Making amends with the Suttons now seemed impossible.

Before this incident occurred, the Suttons had used a logging road that passed near Mrs. Totten's property and ran right through Mrs. Beebe's property. Mrs. Beebe had agreed to let the Suttons use it until she decided she wanted to use the land for something else. After the trouble with the Sutton boys, Mrs. Totten and Mrs. Beebe erected a fence to keep the Sutton family from passing through Mrs. Beebe's property on that road. Mrs. Beebe told Mr. Sutton that if he wished, he could build a new road at a higher location. She wanted to use the old road, which passed through good bottomland, for gardening. He complained because building a new road would be nearly impossible due to the steepness of the slope, but Mrs. Beebe had already given her ultimatum. Will Tabor started clearing the land to be planted while Mrs. Beebe erected a fence and gates. The Suttons continued to pass through on the road, leaving the gates open. Animals came in and ate the produce right out of the garden. When Mrs. Beebe asked the Suttons to shut the gates, they refused. She put a lock on the gate and told the Suttons they could have the key if they asked for it.

Instead of asking for the key, on August 9, the three Sutton brothers wrecked the fence and cut up the No Trespassing sign. Mrs. Beebe was infuriated. The next morning she drove to Cashmere to demand the boys' arrest. She could not find a lawman, so she returned home and went directly to Mrs. Totten's home to tell her what had happened.

They decided to repair the fence. They packed a picnic lunch to take with them, and Mrs. Totten brought her shotgun along. Mrs. Beebe brought the ax she used to chase birds from her fruit trees and her garden. The two women walked to the place where the fence needed to be fixed. After a few hours they finished the job, then sat down several yards away to eat lunch.

Not long afterward, James Sutton approached the fence in his wagon, carrying a load of wood that he was taking to market. He usually took this road to go to town, but Mrs. Totten and Mrs. Beebe had just stretched a fence across it. He asked them to remove it, which they refused to do. Mrs. Totten declared that the Suttons had been told several times that Mrs. Beebe was no longer going to allow the easement through her property for their use. She told Mr. Sutton that he would have to build another road. Mr. Sutton was dismayed by this, but he didn't argue. He unloaded the wood nearby and returned to his home.

Mrs. Totten and Mrs. Beebe thought the matter was settled. But just after four o'clock that afternoon, several of the Sutton children approached in a wagon. The eldest son, Jim, drove the wagon, while Nettie, Milroy, and John rode along. Evidently, their father had told them what had transpired at the fence earlier in the day. Jim walked right up to the fence with an old ax and a blacksmith hammer and started cutting the wires.

Mrs. Totten and Mrs. Beebe were still sitting about fifty feet away. Mrs. Beebe quickly approached Jim Sutton and asked him to stop. She pointed to a NO TRESPASSING sign that the women had just erected, but he didn't even stop his work. He simply replied that he didn't care about the sign. Mrs. Beebe said, "If you don't care about that trespass sign, do you care for that gun?" She started swatting at Sutton's hands with her ax while he worked. He kept right on cutting the wires. Mrs. Totten approached with her gun and said, "Jim Sutton, you're a coward; you would not dare do a thing of this kind to anybody but a woman. You ought to have been in the penitentiary long ago." Nettie spoke up and asked Mrs. Totten what Jim had done that he ought to go to prison. Mrs. Totten told her to shut up or she would shoot her.

Finally Jim Sutton cut through the last of the four wires. Mrs. Totten told her mother to get out of the way so she could shoot him. Jim swung around with his hammer and made a threatening move toward Mrs. Beebe. When Mrs. Totten saw him raise his hand to her mother, she told him to get back or she would shoot him. Jim ducked out of the way and tried to hide behind a stump that was holding the wires. But Mrs. Totten shot him. Nettie screamed when she saw her brother fall. The children jumped out of the buggy and ran up the hill to hide behind the stack of wood their father had left earlier.

Jim Sutton died about fifteen minutes later. The women calmly turned away and walked toward Mrs. Beebe's home, which was about four hundred feet away. The Sutton children drove their wagon home and told their parents what had happened. They alerted the sheriff, who met Mr. Totten on the road coming home from work at a nearby sawmill. The sheriff told him what his wife had done.

When Deputy Bert McManus and Noel Totten arrived at the Totten household, Mrs. Totten had already packed her bags and was waiting for the sheriff to take her to jail. She told her husband that she had just saved the lives of her mother and herself. He replied, "Seems to me you could have saved your lives in some other way without shooting up neighbors."

Deputy McManus drove Mrs. Totten to the jail in his car. Deputy Patton and a newspaper reporter from the *Wenatchee Daily World* named Ellinwood rode along as well. She told both of them that she had killed Jim Sutton to protect her mother.

Mrs. Totten's trial began on November 13. Men named Kemp and Reeves represented the state. Ira Thomas and N. M. Sorenson defended the two women. Judge Grimshaw heard the case. Jury selection took two days because most people had already read the newspaper accounts of the incident so it was difficult to find an impartial jurist. As soon as the jury was picked, they were driven out to the murder site. The defense objected because it was winter and the area looked different than it did at the time of the murder. The defense also felt that Mrs. Totten should be allowed to go too, but she could not because of her delicate health. The judge overruled the defense's objections.

The three Sutton children proved to be very good witnesses. Though young, they were very clear on what had happened. The defense tried to discredit their testimony, but all three told the same story. Thomas was able to get Nettie to admit the family was expecting trouble when they went to the fence site and that they had brought a hammer and ax specifically to cut down the fence.

Noel Totten also testified. He drew a map to show the fences, roads, and corners, in order to show that there were other roads for the Suttons to use to go to Cashmere besides the one going through Mrs. Beebe's property.

Several other witnesses testified that Mrs. Totten's disposition toward the Suttons had not been friendly. She had made disparaging remarks about them in conversation to others and had even threatened them.

Mrs. Totten testified on her own behalf but sounded like she wasn't in her right mind. For example, she related that she had shot Jim Sutton because she felt threatened by him. This was in direct conflict with what she had told deputies immediately after the incident occurred. At that time, she said that she was shooting to save her mother. When the defense asked her to repeat information that she had been asked by the prosecution, she could not always remember what she had already said; other times her remarks were incoherent.

She told how James Sutton had helped her clear some of her property. He had suggested using dynamite to blow up some of the big stumps. She didn't want dynamite being used on her property. She said she felt threatened by him when he said, "You will get blown up by dynamite yourself anyway one of these days." But when she was questioned again by the prosecution, she admitted that she knew Sutton wasn't serious.

Thomas argued eloquently that the two women had only done what anybody else would have done to protect their property. Sutton was trespassing and had repeatedly been warned. He said that Jim Sutton went to the Beebe property that day deliberately to cause mischief. Mrs. Totten only fired in self-defense, he argued.

The jury considered the defense attorney's remarks for twelve hours. At three o'clock in the morning on November 22, the jury reached a decision. Once they agreed on her guilt, they voted nine times before agreeing on the degree of guilt. Court convened at nine o'clock the next morning for the reading of the verdict. Mrs. Totten was pronounced guilty of first-degree murder. She was escorted back to the jail immediately.

The judge called a recess until the afternoon, at which time Mrs. Beebe's trial began. Thomas also represented Mrs. Beebe. There was much more sympathy for Mrs. Beebe, in part due to her age of sixty-nine.

Over the next two days, most of the same witnesses from Mrs. Totten's trial returned to testify again. The Sutton children repeated much of the same information they had already given. Nettie explained the sequence of events leading up to the shooting of Jim Sutton. She also told about hiding behind the woodpile after her brother had been shot.

When Mrs. Beebe testified, she admitted that she attacked Jim Sutton with her ax. But she felt she had a legal right to do so, since he was trespassing on her land. But when she said, "If you don't care about that trespass sign, do you care for that gun?" she certainly encouraged her daughter to shoot, even though she didn't pull the trigger herself. Her statement and the fact that she moved out of the way when Mrs. Totten told her to do so convinced the jury that Mrs. Beebe had some degree of guilt.

The defense made a lengthy closing argument that lasted clear into the next day. Sorenson argued that if the crime was committed in a fit of passion or fear, then she could not have been in her right mind when it occurred, and the jury would have to find her guilty of manslaughter rather than murder. He brought up discrepancies in the testimony and even accused Nettie of telling her younger brothers what to say. He argued that the two women had not gone out to repair the fence with the intent to commit murder.

After the defense rested, the judge instructed the jury on their duty. The jury deliberated for only a few hours. After three votes they reached a unanimous decision. They found Mrs. Beebe guilty of manslaughter.

On December 15, both women were sentenced. Mrs. Beebe was sentenced to at least one year, but not more than two, of hard labor in the state prison. Mrs. Totten seems to have hurt her own cause. Many felt she was contradictory and even seemed vindictive on the stand. At times, she even seemed proud of what she had done. When she was sentenced to life in prison, nobody was particularly surprised, including her husband.

Thomas got both cases before the appeals court. Mrs. Beebe's case was heard in January 1912. The basis of the appeal was that the jury did not receive appropriate instructions and that certain evidence was admitted that prejudiced Mrs. Beebe's case. The court disagreed that the jury instructions were improper, but it did agree that the statements that Mrs. Totten made were irrelevant to Mrs. Beebe's case. The court granted her a new trial on that basis. The outcome of that trial is not known, but presumably most of her time would have been served already by the time of the new trial.

Mrs. Totten wasn't as lucky. The appellate court reaffirmed the decision of the trial court in February of 1912. Thomas used the same arguments: The jury did not receive appropriate instructions and certain evidence was admitted that prejudiced Mrs. Totten's case. But the court disagreed and the decision of the trial court stood. Mrs. Totten began serving her sentence with credit for time already served.

William T. Phillips

This was the end—they were backed up against a wall. Butch Cassidy and the Sundance Kid had just robbed a bank and were on the run. They were hiding out in San Vicente, Bolivia, in South America. Unfortunately a man there noticed they were leading a mule that had been stolen from a friend of his. He alerted the local police, and the police sent soldiers to the place where the mule was seen. The soldiers called out for the men to surrender.

Butch and Sundance hid in a small adobe hut. One of them ran out to the horses to get some rifles for the coming siege. He was fired upon and injured. The other man ran out and was wounded too, though he managed to grab some guns and drag the first man back into the hut. The soldiers decided to rush the hut. Even though there were many more soldiers than robbers, the robbers killed one soldier and wounded several. The gunfire went on until long after dark. Butch and Sundance were running out of ammunition, so they began to ration their shots. Finally, no shots at all came from the hut. But the soldiers didn't trust the wily outlaws and kept firing at the hut all night long.

By the next morning, there were no signs of resistance from inside the hut. The soldiers entered the shelter and found the bodies of both outlaws. It appeared Butch had shot Sundance and then killed himself. The lives of Butch Cassidy and the Sundance Kid were at an end. Or were they?

Throughout the 1890s, Butch Cassidy, the Sundance Kid, and the Wild Bunch had terrorized the mountain states of

America with a series of bold and daring bank robberies and train holdups. But one day Butch and Sundance decided to call it quits. Many of their compatriots had been either killed or captured. They figured the best way to evade the law forever was to leave the country.

So in 1902, Butch, Sundance, and Sundance's girlfriend, Etta Place, left the United States and went to South America. After trying several operations, both legitimate and illegal, they finally ended up in Bolivia, where the two men were hired as security guards at a tin mine.

After a time, the South American police caught up with them at the hut. They were suspected of robbing a pack train carrying the miners' payroll. Instead of surrendering peacefully, Butch and Sundance made a stand. The shoot-out commenced.

But almost as soon as they were dead, rumors began. Their friends back in the States suspected that Butch and Sundance faked their deaths so that they could start new lives elsewhere. Several of them took up a collection and sent a man to South America to investigate whether or not Butch and Sundance were really dead. The man returned with photos of the dead outlaws and stories from soldiers who were there. All evidence pointed to the fact that Butch and Sundance really were dead, although some people claimed the man in the picture wasn't Butch Cassidy.

But in the 1930s serious speculation about the case began. The speculation resulted from the Depression–era project known as the Works Progress Administration. The program was started to employ writers and artists who had lost their jobs because of the Depression. One of the projects the WPA tackled was to write a history of each of the fifty states. When the writers came to Wyoming, they began hearing stories of how Butch Cassidy returned to the United States after he had supposedly died in Bolivia. The old-timers told the government men that they knew that Cassidy was living in Spokane under a different name, but they didn't know what that name was. Research turned up the name William T. Phillips.

Before 1910, Phillips had never set foot in Washington state. In 1908 he had gone to Michigan, where he married Gertrude Livesay. The couple first lived in Globe, Arizona, before moving to Spokane in the winter of 1910. At first he worked for the Washington Water Power Company. A year later he tried prospecting in Alaska but came back when he had no luck.

In 1915 he started the Phillips Manufacturing Company, which invented parts for farm equipment, automatic garage door openers, and gas mileage indicators for cars. He went to the Burroughs Company with his ideas, but they would not pay what he was asking. Since he never patented his ideas, the company simply copied them.

In 1918 Phillips expanded his business to include a machine shop. He moved to a larger building on Division Street. He was doing enough business to employ three other people. In 1925 he moved to a new home on West Providence. The onset of the Depression left in him dire straits, however, and he had to sell the shop to two of his employees because he couldn't pay them.

He was broke, but during the 1920s and 1930s he somehow managed to finance several trips to Wyoming, where he prospected for outlaw loot. From then until his death, he made a living by working odd jobs and selling his inventions. He died on July 20, 1937, after a battle with cancer and was buried at the county poor farm.

At the time of his death, most of the people who knew him believed that Phillips was really Butch Cassidy. Phillips himself claimed to be Butch Cassidy and made no secret of it. Historians and scholars dispute the idea. But if Phillips was not Cassidy, there is certainly enough evidence to prove why the uninitiated believed he was.

For example, the timing of his arrival in Washington coincides nicely with the timing of the shoot-out in Bolivia. Cassidy would have needed several months to make his way back to the States. In addition, no records have been found to prove that William T. Phillips even existed until his marriage was recorded in 1908.

Another interesting fact is that neither the Pinkerton Detective Agency, which was following the Butch and Sundance case, nor Bolivian authorities could ever find any evidence of a shoot-out at San Vicente. Even local citizens of San Vicente who were quizzed about it after the fact did not remember any shoot-out occurring there. Years later, two bodies were exhumed in San Vicente that were supposedly Butch and Sundance. A DNA test proved that two other men were buried in those graves.

Phillips told various business associates and friends that he was the notorious Cassidy. The Lundstrom family, who knew Phillips from about 1914 until his death in 1937, said they were aware of Phillips's true identity almost from the start, although they never talked about it in front of his wife. The family always knew him to be easygoing and good-natured. When Phillips visited their home, he often brought candy or some small gift for their children. Mrs. Lundstrom packed food for Phillips when he took one of his trips to Wyoming. She also took care of him in his last days.

William T. Phillips in his later years.
(Courtesy Jim Dullenty, Hamilton, Montana)

Athol Evans worked for Phillips from 1921 until 1930. When Phillips was forced to sell his shop, Evans and a machinist named Frank Frueschuetz assumed his debts and were able to keep the shop open. One of their largest contracts was the Riblet Tramway Company of Spokane. One day, Riblet offered Phillips a job as a construction superintendent on a tramway in Bolivia. Phillips turned down the offer, even though he needed the money. Evans couldn't figure out why he didn't want to go to Bolivia, so Phillips told him who he really was.

Another friend who wanted to remain anonymous accompanied Phillips on one of his trips to Wyoming in the 1930s. He said many old-timers greeted Phillips as Cassidy, and the man was pretty well convinced that Phillips really was Cassidy.

Phillips had prospected along the Columbia River near Daisy, Washington, and several people there knew Phillips as Butch Cassidy. Dan Parker, Butch Cassidy's brother, also believed that Phillips was really Cassidy. Phillips visited Parker in Milford, Utah, in 1930. Parker's wife, Ellnor, and son Max were there at the time, and they all thought that Phillips was Cassidy. After the visit, the two men regularly exchanged letters.

Cassidy's sister, Lula Parker Betenson, admitted that her brother had come home and visited his family in Utah in 1925, proving that Cassidy had survived the Bolivia shoot-out. In a 1970 interview, she said the whole family agreed to keep his secret. But when Betenson wrote her own book about her outlaw brother and published it in 1973, she denied that Phillips was Cassidy. But because she changed her story each time she was interviewed, people began to believe what they wanted to believe.

Phillips's wife, Gertrude, and his adopted son, William R., also believed that he was really Butch Cassidy, even though Gertrude would deny it when asked. William R. Phillips said that she denied it because she was embarrassed by it and because she did not want her son to grow up under the stigma of being an outlaw's son. But William R. always knew it to be true and had always thought that he was the adopted son of a once-famous outlaw who had gone straight.

Mary Boyd was a onetime sweetheart of Butch Cassidy. He had intended to marry her but had had to flee the law instead. Boyd had recently been widowed when Phillips came to Wyoming in 1934. She immediately recognized Phillips as her old sweetheart. They corresponded regularly after that.

When Phillips took his many trips to the Rocky Mountain country, he was greeted by several old acquaintances there who knew him in the early part of the twentieth century. In 1922 John Taylor reported that Butch Cassidy came to his garage in Rock Springs, Wyoming, to get his car repaired. He didn't tell Taylor who he was, but Taylor was sure he was Cassidy. Two years later, Tom Welch of Green River, Wyoming, visited with Cassidy. Welch said that Cassidy was driving the same Model T he had had fixed in Rock Springs and was traveling under an assumed name. In 1925 Phillips visited his old friend Bert Charter in Jackson Hole, Wyoming. Charter later told his friend Will Simpson, the prosecuting attorney at Cassidy's 1894 trial, about the visit, and they talked as if the man really was Cassidy. Tom Vernon, the mayor of Baggs, Wyoming, also claimed to have seen Cassidy in the mid-1920s.

Ellen Harris and her son accompanied Phillips on one of his trips to Wyoming. They met Phillips at the Hotel Utah in Salt

Lake City. Then they drove on to Rock Springs and Lander, Wyoming. Phillips was going prospecting for a gold deposit that an old Indian named Whiskey Jack had told him about. While in Lander, the group met several people who recognized Phillips as Cassidy. Some people at Fort Washakie also acknowledged Phillips as Cassidy.

There was physical evidence, too. As soon as he returned from his unsuccessful trip to Lander, Phillips wrote a manuscript he called The Bandit Invincible. Ellen Harris typed it up for him. The manuscript had many details that only the real Butch Cassidy would have known. For example, the manuscript told about the last battle between Cassidy and the Bolivian troops. He included many details about Bolivia that could not have been known by the average American. The manuscript explained how Cassidy finally escaped, sailed to Paris for plastic surgery, then returned to the United States and was married. This story also explained why Phillips's appearance was slightly different from remembered pictures of Cassidy.

Researcher Larry Pointer found some old letters that Phillips had written to his old girlfriend, Mary Boyd. He also found a letter known to have been written by Cassidy. He hired handwriting analysis expert Jeannine Zimmerman to compare the two letters. Her conclusion was that even given the differences naturally caused by age, the two letters could have come from the same hand. She said that the two penmanship samples had some very unusual similarities, and the two letters shared a consistent writing style.

When Larry Pointer published a book about the mystery surrounding Butch Cassidy and the Sundance Kid, William R. Phillips was working as a handyman and custodian in Spokane.

Pointer designated that part of the royalties from his book go toward helping Phillips. Evidently, Pointer was convinced.

Shortly before he died, Phillips secretly sent Mary Boyd an unusual ring with a Mexican fire opal. He had written to her about the ring in December 1935. After Phillips died, Boyd wrote a letter to William L. Fields in Spokane, who knew about their relationship. She told him about the ring that Phillips had worn for fifty-five years and then had given to her just before he died. Inside the band was an inscription that read "Geo C to Mary B." Could this inscription be short for "George Cassidy to Mary Boyd"? George Cassidy was the name Cassidy was using at the time the ring was made.

Roy Jones and Herman LaJeunesse, nephews of Will Boyd, Mary's brother, positively identified some pictures as being those of Butch Cassidy. Among the pictures were some known to be William Phillips. The nephews had seen Cassidy frequently when he had courted Mary. They also had a letter that Ellen Harris wrote to them. She was also positive that Phillips was Cassidy.

Phillips owned a .22 Derringer and two Colt revolvers. On the handle of one of the guns was a distinguishing mark that was an exact duplicate of a cattle brand once used by Cassidy.

All these arguments seem pretty convincing. But there was just as much evidence to suggest that Phillips wasn't Cassidy. Historian Jim Dullenty only needed one piece of evidence to convince him the two men were not the same. How could a relatively uneducated and unskilled man such as Butch Cassidy operate a successful machine shop for close to twenty years?

Other discrepancies in his background also dispute some of the so-called positive evidence. For example, his application to the Spokane Elks and Masonic lodges said he was born in

Sandusky, Michigan. But in 1865, when he was born, the town of Sandusky did not exist. He listed his parents as Laddie J. and Celia Mudge Phillips, but there are no records in Michigan of either name. There were also no records to show that Laddie Phillips ever paid taxes, voted, or owned property between 1860 and 1870. Phillips claimed he operated a machine shop in Des Moines, Iowa, yet there are no listings for his business between 1900 and 1908, when he allegedly lived there.

A William Phillips is listed in a Des Moines, Iowa, directory in 1896 as an insurance salesman. If it was the same Phillips, then Phillips could not possibly be the outlaw because the real Cassidy had just been released from a Wyoming prison on January 19, 1896.

Another inconsistency is the fact that Phillips had several female relationships. In addition to his wife, there was a woman named Anna Galusha, who was a detective in a Spokane department store. Apparently he also had a common-law wife on the Wind River Indian Reservation in Wyoming, whom he visited when he went there in 1933. Then there was Mary Boyd, the woman who received his old ring. The real Cassidy was never known to have been married or to even have had a steady relationship with anyone.

Researcher Charles Kelly was working on the first edition of his book *The Outlaw Trail* when he heard about the controversy surrounding Butch Cassidy's death. Despite his doubts, he decided to look into it. He ordered a copy of Phillips's death certificate from the Washington State Bureau of Vital Statistics. The fact that the death certificate said Phillips's birthplace was Michigan was enough to convince him Phillips was a phony. The real Butch Cassidy was born in Utah.

Kelly wrote to Gertrude Phillips to ask her about the rumors. She would only admit that Phillips had ridden with Cassidy. She gave him enough details for Kelly to believe that Phillips had known Cassidy, but not that he was him.

Some others who had known Cassidy believed that Phillips was not him. Rancher Jim Regan had known Cassidy in his early days. He said that Phillips was taller and heavier than Cassidy. The known height of Cassidy was five feet, nine inches tall, while Phillips was five feet, ten or eleven inches tall. The Rife brothers from Mt. Carmel, Utah, said that Phillips often posed as Cassidy just for fun.

Other handwriting experts looked at the two letters, one from Phillips and one from Cassidy, and could not be as definitive as Zimmerman was. One expert said the letters were definitely written by two different people. The other could not make a decision one way or the other.

Researchers Dan Buck and Anne Meadows were able to come up with a photo of Phillips's mother, Celia Mudge. There was so much resemblance between her and Phillips, they figured she had to be his real mother. This meant there was no way that Annie Gillies Parker, Butch Cassidy's mother, was Phillips's mother. For them the question was resolved when they saw that picture. Computerized photo analysis at the Los Alamos National Laboratory and at the University of Illinois at Chicago solidified their opinions.

William T. Phillips died before anyone questioned him extensively about his past. The Masonic Lodge held a service for him after his death. His wife scattered his ashes over the Little Spokane River, as Phillips had wished. She held various jobs until the early 1950s, when she retired. She died of cancer on April 16, 1959.

Whether or not Butch Cassidy survived the Bolivia shoot-out and later lived in Washington state is still highly disputed even by professional researchers. Still, fans of Old West literature prefer to think that both men survived the shoot-out and went on to lead ordinary, law-abiding lives. Maybe they did.

Bibliography

Lawrence Kelly

New York Times, "A Smuggler Captured; Taken With Sixty-Five Cans of Opium in His Possession," March 15, 1891.

Seattle Post-Intelligencer, May 15, 1909.

Clark, Cecil. *The Daily Colonist*. April 8, 1962.

Cummings, Jo Bailey, and Al Cummings. *San Juan: The Powder Keg Island*. Friday Harbor, WA: Beach Combers, 1987.

Davenport, Marge. *Afloat and Awash in the Old Northwest*. Tigard, OR: Paddlewheel Press, 1988.

Dirks, Farmer. "Ship Owned by Pirate Kelly Discovered Here." *American Bulletin*. Anacortes, WA, September 2, 1955.

———. "Case of Missing Tools When Kelly Was Alive." *American Bulletin*. Anacortes, WA, September 9, 1955.

———. "Smuggler Kelly a Bad One, But Paid His Debts." *American Bulletin*. Anacortes, WA, September 12, 1955.

Jones, Roy Franklin. *Boundary Town: Early Days in a Northwest Boundary Town*. Vancouver: Fleet Printing Company, 1958.

McCurdy, James G. "Criss-Cross Over the Boundary: The Romance of Smuggling across the Northwest Frontier." Portland, OR: *The Pacific Monthly*, Volume XXIII, January to June 1910.

McDonald, Lucille S. "Kelly, the King of the Smugglers, Guemes, Sinclair Islands were headquarters of notorious operator in years long past." *Seattle Times*, March 29, 1959.

———. *Making History: The People who Shaped the San Juan Islands*. Friday Harbor, WA: Harbor Press, 1990.

———. "Old records tell how Puget Sound customs men went about tracking the smugglers." *Seattle Times*, July 27, 1952.

Richardson, David. *Pig War Islands*. Eastsound, WA: Orcas Publishing Company, 1971.

Short, E. T. "The End of Lawrence Kelly." *Tacoma Times*.

Telephone interview with Pat Nelson, great-granddaughter of Lawrence Kelly, August 18, 2000.

The Roslyn Bank Robbery

Ellensburg Daily Record, "Memoirs of Bandit Rider Jobs Pioneers' Recollection of Roslyn Bank Robbery," February 10, 1938.

New York Times, "A Bold Bank Robbery," September 26, 1892.

Sheller, Roscoe. *Bandit to Lawman*. Yakima, WA: Franklin Press, Inc., 1966.

———. *Ben Snipes, Northwest Cattle King*. Portland, OR: Binford & Mort Publishing, 1957.

Smokov, Mark T. "The Bank Robbery at Roslyn, Washington." *The Journal*. Helena, MT: Western-Outlaw Lawman Association, Spring 1999.

Spawn of Coal Dust: History of Roslyn 1886–1955. A Project of Operation Uplift Community Program, Roslyn, WA, 1955.

Warner, Matt, as told to Murray E. King. *The Last of the Bandit Riders.* New York: Bonanza Books, 1940.

Johnny Schnarr

Mortenson, Lynn Ove. "Black nights and bootleg booze." Peninsula Magazine. Summer, 1993.

Newsome, Eric. *Pass the Bottle: Rum Tales of the West Coast.* Victoria, BC: Orca Book Publishing, 1995.

Parker, Marion and Robert Tyrell. *Rumrunner: The Life and Times of Johnny Schnarr.* Victoria, BC: Orca Book Publishing, 1988.

Thomas Blanck

Seattle Post-Intelligencer, October 1, 1894.

Seattle Post-Intelligencer, October 2, 1894.

Seattle Post-Intelligencer, October 3, 1894.

Seattle Post-Intelligencer, October 4, 1894.

Seattle Post-Intelligencer, October 5, 1894.

Seattle Post-Intelligencer, October 6, 1894.

Seattle Post-Intelligencer, October 7, 1894.

Seattle Post-Intelligencer, October 18, 1894.

Seattle Post-Intelligencer, October 19, 1894.

Seattle Post-Intelligencer, October 23, 1894.

Seattle Post-Intelligencer, October 24, 1894.

Seattle Post-Intelligencer, December 11, 1894.

Seattle Post-Intelligencer, March 18, 1895.

Seattle Post-Intelligencer, March 19, 1895.

Seattle Post-Intelligencer, March 20, 1895.

Seattle Post-Intelligencer, March 21, 1895.

Seattle Post-Intelligencer, March 22, 1895.

Seattle Post-Intelligencer, March 23, 1895.

McClary, Daryl C. "Outlaw Thomas Blanck shoots and skills Charles H. Bridwell during a robbery in Seattle on October 3, 1894," HistoryLink.org, March 23, 2010. www.historylink.org/index.cfm?DisplayPage=output .cfm&file_id=9358

McClary, Daryl C., "Condemned murderer Thomas Blanck escapes from the King County Jail on March 17, 1895," HistoryLink.org, May 12, 2010. www.historylink.org/ index.cfm?DisplayPage=output.cfm&file_id=9391

Frank Leroy

Okanogan Independent, November 12, 1909.

Okanogan Independent, November 17, 1909.

Okanogan Independent, November 26, 1909.

Okanogan Record (Conconully), November 26, 1909.

Getty, Mona. "Fred Thorp, Sheriff of Okanogan County." Okanogan County Heritage. Okanogan, WA: Okanogan County Historical Society, Inc., March 1966.

Wilson, Bruce A. *Late Frontier, A History of Okanogan County, Washington (1800–1941)*. Okanogan, WA: Okanogan County Historical Society, Inc., 1990.

61 Wash. 405, State v. Leroy.

John Tornow

Aberdeen Daily World, September 8, 1911–September 9, 1911.

Aberdeen Daily World, August 14, 1912.

Aberdeen Daily World, May 30, 1987.

Aberdeen Herald, March 21, 1912.

Bristow, Allen P. "Phantom of the Forest." *True West Magazine*. Stillwater, OK: Western Publications, August 1999.

Fowler, Ron. *Guilty by Circumstance*. Steilacoom, WA: Fowler Freelance, 1997.

Fultz, Hollis B. *Famous Northwest Manhunts and Murder Mysteries*. Elma, WA: Fulco Publications, 1955.

Hillier, Alfred J. "John Tornow, the Outlaw Hermit." *Pacific Northwest Quarterly*. Seattle: University of Washington, July 1944.

Hughes, John C., and Ryan Teague Beckwirth, editors. *On the Harbor: From Black Friday to Nirvania*. Las Vegas: Stephens Press LLC, 2005.

Lindstrom, Bill. "John Tornow: The legend lives after 75 years, but many questions are still unanswered." *Aberdeen Daily World*, April 16, 1988.

———. "John Tornow: The manhunt begins: In the next 19 months only the woods knew the real story." *Aberdeen Daily World*, April 17, 1988.

———. "Wildman of the Wynooche." *Peninsula Magazine*.

Lucia, Ellis. *Tough Men, Tough Country*. Englewood Cliffs, NJ: Prentice Hall, 1963.

Shields, Mike. "Terror in the Mist." *True West Magazine*. Austin: Western Publications, Inc., January/February 1967.

Unpublished transcription of interview of Dan McGillicuddy,
from shorthand notes taken by Anne Cotton, August 23,
1971, courtesy Aberdeen Public Library.

Van Syckle, Edwin. *The River Pioneers, Early Days on Grays
Harbor.* Seattle: Pacific Search Press, 1982.

The Great Nude Bathing Case

Tacoma Tribune, November 7, 1911.

Tacoma Tribune, January 11, 1912–January 14, 1912.

*Along the Waterfront, A History of the Gig Harbor and Key
Peninsula Areas.* Compiled and written by 1974–1975
students of Goodman Middle School, Gig Harbor, WA:
Clinton-Hull Printing Company, Ltd., 1979.

Florin, Lambert. *Ghost Towns of the West.* New York:
Promontory Press, 1993.

Holbrook, Stewart. *Little Annie Oakley and Other Rugged
People.* New York: MacMillan Company, 1948, originally
printed in *The American Scholar,* 1946.

Morgan, Murray. *Last Wilderness.* New York: Viking Press,
1955.

71 Wash. 185, State v. Fox.

Harry Tracy

Centralia News-Examiner, July 18, 1902.

Chehalis Bee Nuggett, July 11, 1902.

Davenport Times-Tribune, July 8, 1954.

Lewis County Advocate (Chehalis), July 18, 1902.

Dullenty, Jim. *Harry Tracy: The Last Desperado*. Dubuque, IA: Kendall/Hunt Publishing Company, 1996.

Fultz, Hollis B. *Famous Northwest Manhunts and Murder Mysteries*. Elma, WA: Fulco Publications, 1955.

Gulick, Bill. Manhunt: *The Pursuit of Harry Tracy*. Caldwell, ID: Caxton Press, 1999.

History of the Big Bend Country. Spokane: Western Historical Publishing Co., 1904.

Horan, James D. *The Outlaws*. New York: Random House, 1977.

Lucia, Ellis. *Tough Men, Tough Country*. Englewood Cliffs, NJ: Prentice Hall, 1963.

Raine, William MacLeod. *Famous Sheriffs and Western Outlaws*. New York: Doubleday & Company, Inc., 1929.

Sifakis, Carl. *Encyclopedia of American Crime*. New York: Facts on File, Inc., 1982.

Wismer, F. D., and Ellison, Douglas W., ed. *The Life of Harry Tracy, The Convict Outlaw*. Medora, ND: Dacotah Publishing Company, 1990. Reprint of the 1902 edition.

Shoot-Out at Kennewick

Kennewick Courier, November 2, 1906.

Kennewick Courier, November 9, 1906.

Kennewick Courier, November 5, 1931.

Prosser Bulletin, November 1, 1906.

Prosser Bulletin, November 8, 1906.

Prosser Bulletin, November 15, 1906.

Prosser Bulletin, November 29, 1906.

Prosser Bulletin, January 3, 1907.

Prosser Bulletin, January 10, 1907.

Prosser Bulletin, January 17, 1907.

Tri-City Herald (Kennewick), September 3, 1978.

Dullenty, Jim. "Shootout at Poplar Grove." *True West Magazine*. Iola, WI: Western Publications, January 1984.

Gibson, Beth. "This and That." *The Courier*. Kennewick, WA: East Benton County Historical Society, April 1996.

Mercer, Tom. "Lawmen Honored." *The Courier*. Kennewick, WA: East Benton County Historical Society, June 1998.

Parker, Martha Berry. *Kin-I-wak, Kenewick, Tehe, Kennewick*. Fairfield, WA: Ye Galleon Press, 1986.

Patterson, Richard. *Historical Atlas of the Outlaw West*. Boulder, CO: Johnson Publishing Company, 1985.

Peter Miller

Seattle Post-Intelligencer, November 28, 1908–December 4, 1908.

Seattle Post-Intelligencer, December 8, 1908.

Seattle Post-Intelligencer, April 27, 1909.

Seattle Post-Intelligencer, October 30, 1909–November 4, 1909.

Seattle Post-Intelligencer, November 28, 1909.

Seattle Post-Intelligencer, November 30, 1909.

Seattle Post-Intelligencer, February 20, 1913.

Spokesman Review, November 7, 1909.

Fultz, Hollis B. *Famous Northwest Manhunts and Murder Mysteries*. Elma, WA: Fulco Publications, 1955.

61 Wash. 125, State v. Miller.

68 Wash. 239, State v. Miller.

72 Wash. 154, State v. Miller.

78 Wash. 268, State v. Miller.

Lum You

South Bend Journal, July 6, 1894.

South Bend Journal, July 13, 1894.

South Bend Journal, August 9, 1901.

South Bend Journal, October 18, 1901.

South Bend Journal, October 25, 1901.

South Bend Journal, November 15, 1901.

South Bend Journal, January 17, 1902.

South Bend Journal, January 31, 1902.

Clark, Hope Wilson. "The Bay Center Story." *The Sou'wester.*
Raymond, WA: Pacific County Historical Society, Inc.,
Spring 1971.

Dixon, Ruth. "Invitation to a Hanging." *The Sou'wester.*
Raymond, WA: Pacific County Historical Society, Inc.,
Spring 1971.

William Frederick Jahns

Spokesman Review, October 30, 1909–October 31, 1909.

Spokesman Review, November 4, 1909–November 7, 1909.

Spokesman Review, January 2, 1910–January 4, 1910.

Spokesman Review, January 9, 1910.

Spokesman Review, January 12, 1910–January 22, 1910.

Fultz, Hollis B. *Famous Northwest Manhunts and Murder
Mysteries.* Elma, WA: Fulco Publications, 1955.

Rustlers!

Kennewick Courier, July 27, 1906.

Kennewick Reporter, March 27, 1908.

Kennewick Reporter, April 28, 1908.

Prosser Bulletin, July 19, 1906.

Prosser Bulletin, July 26, 1906.

Seattle Post-Intelligencer, July 21, 1909–July 25, 1909.

Twin City Reporter (Kennewick), July 14, 1909.

Walla Walla Evening Bulletin, July 27, 1906.

Walla Walla Evening Bulletin, March 28, 1908.

Walla Walla Evening Bulletin, April 21, 1908–April 23, 1908.

Brown, Joseph C., editor. *The Night the Mountain Fell and Other Stories of North Central Washington History.* Wenatchee, WA: A KPQ Publication, 1973.

Hormel, Monty. *The Old West in Grant County.* Ephrata, WA: Tamanawahs Publications, 1990.

Kuykendall, Elgin V. *History of Garfield County.* Fairfield, WA: Ye Galleon Press, 1984.

Walter, Edward M. and Susan A. Fleury. *Eureka Gulch: The Rush for Gold, A History of Republic Mining Camp, 1896–1908.* Colville, WA: Don's Printery, 1985.

Max Levy

Port Townsend Daily Leader, August 12, 1893.

Port Townsend Daily Leader, August 13, 1893.

Port Townsend Daily Leader, August 15, 1893.

Port Townsend Daily Leader, August 16, 1893.

Port Townsend Daily Leader, August 24, 1893.

Port Townsend Daily Leader, September 13, 1893.

Port Townsend Daily Leader, September 24, 1893.

Port Townsend Daily Leader, November 15, 1893.

Port Townsend Daily Leader, November 16, 1893.

Port Townsend Morning Leader, May 19, 1896.

Port Townsend Morning Leader, May 21, 1896.

Port Townsend Morning Leader, May 23, 1896.

Port Townsend Morning Leader, April 6, 1906.

Port Townsend Leader, August 28, 1996.

Seattle Times. September 9, 1962.

Canfield, Thomas W. *Port Townsend, An Illustrated History of Shanghaiing, Shipwrecks, Soiled Doves, and Sundry Souls.* Port Townsend, WA: Ah Tom Publishing, Inc., 2000.

Dillon, Richard H. *Shanghaiing Days.* New York: Coward-McCann, Inc., 1962.

Newell, Gordon. "Maritime Events of 1903." H.W. *McCurdy Marine History of the Pacific Northwest.* Seattle: Superior Publishing Company, 1966.

Newell, Gordon. *Sea Rogue's Gallery.* Seattle: Superior Publishing Company, 1971.

Simpson, Peter. *City of Dreams, A Guide to Port Townsend.* Port Townsend: The Bay Press, 1986.

Roy Olmstead

Seattle Daily Times, January 20, 1925–January 22, 1925.

Seattle Daily Times, February 2, 1926–February 9, 1926.

Seattle Daily Times, March 10, 1926.

Clark, Norman H. "A Booze Baron's Flamboyant Reign." *Seattle Magazine,* September, 1964.

———. *The Dry Years, Prohibition and Social Change in Washington.* Seattle: University of Washington Press, 1988.

———. "Roy Olmstead, A Rumrunning King on Puget Sound." *Pacific Northwest Quarterly.* Seattle: University of Washington, July 1963.

McClary, Daryl C., "Olmstead, Roy (1886–1966)— King of King County Bootleggers," HistoryLink .org, November 12, 2002. www.historylink.org/index .cfm?DisplayPage=output.cfm&file_id=4015

Newell, Gordon. *Sea Rogues Gallery.* Seattle: Superior Publishing Company, 1971.

Newsome, Eric. *Pass the Bottle: Rum Tales of the West Coast.* Victoria, BC: Orca Book Publishing, 1995.

Olmstead v. United States, 277 US 438, 487–488.

Richardson, David. *Pig War Islands.* Eastsound, WA: Orcas Publishing Company, 1971.

The 1905 Great Northern Train Robbery

Seattle Post-Intelligencer, October 3, 1905–October 7, 1905.

Anderson, Frank W. *Bill Miner: Stagecoach & Train Robber.* Surrey, BC: Heritage House Publishing Co., Ltd., 1982.

Dugan, Mark, and John Boeseneckker. *The Grey Fox: The True Story of Bill Miner—Last of the Old Time Bandits.* Norman, OK: University of Oklahoma Press, 1992.

Rickards, Colin. "Bill Miner—Fifty Years a Holdup Man—
    Conclusion." *Real West Magazine*. Derby, CT: Charlton
    Publications, Inc., October 1970.
Story of Bill Miner, www.rcmp-grc.gc.ca/hist/hh-ps/miner-
    eng.htm, Royal Canadian Mounted Police, May 31, 2010.

Jake Terry

Bellingham Bay Express, July 28, 1891.
Bellingham Bay Express, July 30, 1891.
Seattle Post-Intelligencer, July 5, 1907–July 6, 1907.
Seattle Post-Intelligencer, October 6, 1905.
Dugan, Mark. *Tales Never Told Around the Campfire*. Athens,
    OH: Swallow Press/Ohio University Press, 1992.
Dugan, Mark, and John Boeseneckker. *The Grey Fox: The
    True Story of Bill Miner—Last of the Old Time Bandits*.
    Norman, OK: University of Oklahoma Press, 1992.
Jones, Roy Franklin. *Boundary Town: Early Days in a
    Northwest Boundary Town*. Vancouver: Fleet Printing
    Company, 1958.

Billy Gohl

Grays Harbor Post, June 1, 1907.
Grays Harbor Post, July 6, 1907.
Grays Harbor Washingtonian, March 20, 1910.
Grays Harbor Washingtonian, April 6, 1910.
Grays Harbor Washingtonian, May 4, 1910–May 5, 1910.

Aho, Pamela Dean. "Billy was the Ghoul of Grays Harbor." *The Daily World*. Aberdeen, WA, July 29, 1989.

Betts, William J. "Launched 100 Murders." *Golden West Magazine*. Freeport, NY: Maverick Publications, Inc., January 1970.

Delanty, H. M. *Along the Waterfront, Covering a Period of Fifty Years on Grays Harbor and the Pacific Northwest*. Aberdeen, WA: Quick Print Company, 1943.

Fultz, Hollis B. *Famous Northwest Manhunts and Murder Mysteries*. Elma, WA: Fulco Publications, 1955.

Hughes, John C. and Ryan Teague Beckwith, editors. *On the Harbor: From Black Friday to Nirvana*. Las Vegas: Stephens Press LLC, 2005.

Lind, C. J. "The Port of Missing Men." *Tacoma News-Tribune*. February 23, 1969.

Morgan, Murray. *Last Wilderness*. New York: Viking Press, 1955.

Patterson, Richard. *Historical Atlas of the Outlaw West*. Boulder, CO: Johnson Publishing Company, 1985.

Van Syckle, Edwin. *The River Pioneers, Early Days on Grays Harbor*. Seattle: Pacific Search Press, 1982.

———. *They Tried to Cut it All*. Seattle: Pacific Search Press, 1980.

The Cashmere Fence Dispute

Seattle Post-Intelligencer, November 19, 1910.

Seattle Post-Intelligencer, November 23, 1910.

Seattle Post-Intelligencer, December 4, 1910.

Wenatchee Daily World, November 14, 1910–November 22, 1910.

Wenatchee Daily World, November 26, 1910.

Wenatchee Daily World, November 28, 1910–November 30, 1910.

Wenatchee Daily World, December 2, 1910.

Wenatchee Daily World, December 16, 1910–December 17, 1910.

66 Wash. 463, State v. Beebe.

67 Wash. 192, State v. Totten.

William T. Phillips

Baker, Pearl. *The Wild Bunch at Robbers Roost*. New York: Abelard-Schuman, 1971.

Dullenty, Jim. "Did Butch Cassidy Die in Spokane: Differing Stories Cloud Outlaw's Fate." *Spokane Daily Chronicle*, August 18, 1973.

———. "Did Butch Cassidy Die in Spokane: Summary Leans Toward 'Yes' Answer." *Spokane Daily Chronicle*, September 15, 1973.

———. "Did Butch Cassidy Survive and Live in Spokane?" *The News Tribune*. Tacoma, WA, September 23, 1973.

Kelly, Charles. *The Outlaw Trail: A History of Butch Cassidy & His Wild Bunch*. Lincoln, NE: University of Nebraska Press, 1996. Reprint from the 1958 edition.

Meadows, Anne. *Digging up Butch and Sundance*. New York: St. Martin's Press, 1994.

Netzley, Patricia. *Mysterious Deaths—Butch Cassidy*. San
   Diego: Lucent Books, 1997.
Pointer, Larry. *In Search of Butch Cassidy*. Norman, OK:
   University of Oklahoma Press, 1977.
Schmeltzer, Michael. "Was This Spokane Businessman Really
   Butch Cassidy?" *Spokesman Review*, March 22, 1987.

Index

About the Author

Elizabeth Gibson got hooked on reading and writing at about the age of thirteen. She became interested in history when she read the "Bicentennial Series" by John Jakes. In college she combined these interests as she pursued a double major in English and history. Elizabeth began a career as a freelancer when she researched place name origins in eastern Washington. Her articles have appeared in several local publications and online. She has worked as a technical writer for a government contractor for more than fifteen years. She currently resides in Kennewick, Washington.